T0209406

FLOAT *Your* BOAT

YOU HAVE POWER AND CONTROL

UMAR SIDDIQUI

iUniverse®

FLOAT YOUR BOAT
YOU HAVE POWER AND CONTROL

iUniverse books may be ordered through booksellers or by contacting:

iUniverse
1663 Liberty Drive
Bloomington, IN 47403
www.iuniverse.com
844-349-9409

Because of the dynamic nature of the Internet, any web addresses or links contained in this book may have changed since publication and may no longer be valid. The views expressed in this work are solely those of the author and do not necessarily reflect the views of the publisher, and the publisher hereby disclaims any responsibility for them.

Any people depicted in stock imagery provided by Getty Images are models, and such images are being used for illustrative purposes only.
Certain stock imagery © Getty Images.

ISBN: 978-1-6632-4905-0 (sc)
ISBN: 978-1-6632-4906-7 (e)

Library of Congress Control Number: 2022923075

Print information available on the last page.

iUniverse rev. date: 12/15/2022

CONTENTS

PREFACE

What I have always failed to comprehend and process is how mental health has a stigma. I proudly conquered my schizoaffective bipolar disorder, and most of the people in my life know I have it. Therapy should not be avoided or pathologized. It is therapeutic to "talk it all out" with a therapist; it is an outlet. I did not write this because of a single reason; I have multiple reasons writing a therapy book. I have a master's degree is in mass communication only—that's right, no master's in social work or similar degree. Keep in mind that this is not a manual on therapy on either side—either patients or practitioners—and I am not claiming to be an expert in the field at all. That is a disclaimer to reaffirm the fact that you should take my words as advice and reflections; they are merely anecdotal, not factual.

I think anyone who is an empath could write therapeutically—not necessarily write a book, which might be a little ambitious. I remember how empowered I felt when I self-published a book each time on Amazon. I want to help others, like I always have wanted to, in a prominent way. In this book, I want to be an advocate on many things I am passionate about. I want to inquire and provide insightful answers (subjective answers). I want to be a guiding light; if someone (I cannot recall if anyone has) called me his or her guiding light, I would be elated on many levels, not just flattered.

Creativity is not an inert process; it is a process that is alert. An active and reflexive process, it requires us to be observant. According to Tina Seeling, in her TED Talk "Crash Course in Creativity," we do not teach people how to increase imagination. We need to not think of creativity, or being creative, myopically; we need to view it in another light, if not more than one.[1]

I also feel it is important to pursue your passions—immerse yourself in them. It is harmless; what is the worst the can happen?

---

[1] Tina Seelig, "A Crash Course in Creativity," filmed August 2012 at TEDxStanford, Stanford, CA, video, 18:15, https://www.youtube.com/watch?v=gyM6rx69iqg.

There's always an insistent voice in me that urges me to return to my happy place and reconnect with that which I am passionate about: chiefly Disney and fashion. Of course, I love reading and writing. I am also passionate about the beach and recently have delved into working out more deeply. It is just what makes me feel elated, not just good, that I am always gravitating towards. I want to transcend the mundane at times. I know that may be a banal statement nowadays, since it is normal to want to escape reality with all the disasters and COVID imposing itself upon the world.

An example I always (without fail) think of that always comes to mind for me is Walt Disney and space. I read Neal Gabler's biography of Disney and watched the series *Behind the Attraction* on Disney Plus. Both state that Disney was fascinated by space to the point where it appeared frequently in his visions and parks.[2]

The reason this book exists—the moral or the purpose—is not just to enlighten. It is to *enliven*. Until you know you are living and thriving, you have not completely accomplished this. It is ongoing and takes work. It is human work that is corollary and connected, but usually treated somewhat as ancillary to livelihood. The work must be put in, as with school, work, writing or annotating a book, or in a relationship. The bottom line is that life takes work—meticulous, devoted work.

I also wrote this book with two concepts incessantly pressing and compelling me. First is the fact that creativity has endless potential to help us transcend ourselves. It has the power to make us realize the bigger picture of life and to make us see revelations. The other concept is that we are more alike than different. If we empirically aren't, at least we are focusing on that idea inexplicably more than we should. We ought to stop isolating ourselves, polarizing the world, and creating more dividing lines—for the world is borderless and modern. We need to stop second-guessing that.

---

[2] *Behind the Attraction*, episode 5, "Space Mountain," directed by Brian Volk-Weiss, aired July 21, 2021, on DisneyPlus, https://www.disneyplus.com/video/cd1da80e-09c2-4b5d-b0bc-7dd8f3be648f.

INTRODUCTION

You can find solace in being innovative or creative. Never forget how imperative it is to intertwine creativity with therapy. You are your own protagonist and can provide your own therapy. Before you are therapeutic to others, even on a mass scale, you must take care of yourself. The clichés go on, but you, so to speak, put on your own mask first. It is your equipment to make you sufficient to perform, so to speak, therapy.

Creativity is not strict, monolithic, myopic, or rigid. It is expansive, multifaceted, and has abundant potential. Creativity is not bound by forms or shapes and takes on a fluid livelihood. It manifests itself in our lifespans and is our purpose in many ways. It is not only our purpose, but it is what is endowed upon us. Let me pose a question: is inventing such a daunting feat then so incomprehensible, or are we all inventors? I say that we are all visionaries.

It is important to both recognize and unlock this inventive nature. It is part of us and is given to us, once again.

Creativity is your destiny; it is your journey but also the end result. Creativity is predestined for you; it is preordained. It is more of an endowment, aptitude, and opportunity that is recurrent and innate than a weight that we carry, even though it is a responsibility of sorts. One must harness the power of creativity. It is a gift, and as the clichéd notion says, with it comes (ample) responsibility. Part of this responsibility is recognizing and keeping your self-worth, self-efficacy, and not letting your perception be rigid and monolithic. Creativity is so multifaceted and helps you explore uncharted and challenging territories. It is an indispensable tool to break away from tradition and the mundane as well. We'll get into tradition later, as I tend to and will keep on mentioning it. Let's explore some of the most prominent definitions and characteristics of creativity and its tenets. It is not the first time this will come up, but humans are mind, body, and spirit. They are embodied and disembodied and are souls. These all interlace to compose the person in all of their personhood.

This life is fraught, weighted, multilayered, and multifaceted, and it is important to capture it in whatever form you prefer. Capturing life's intricacies shows effective and engaging vulnerability and is empowering. I capture this through writing and poetry, but whatever artistic outlet or venue is your strong point, go with that. I promise— the general idea of being creative is rooted in you and is immanent to you; you just have to patiently and actively unlock it.

The Human Condition

Before we delve into therapy, we must define and delineate what human nature and the human condition is general. We know the nature versus nurture debate. In an art class, I studied Maurice Merleau-Ponty and John F. Bannan's ideas on phenomenology and how our experiences make us. I have studied Max Wertheimer's ideas on gestalt. We know how John Locke characterized human nature as a blank slate, according to Nicholas G. Petryszak.[3] In a book I am reading, *Dress Codes: How the Laws of Fashion Made History* by Richard Thompson Ford, he says, "We have replaced the concept of sin with the idea of malice, the confessional booth with the therapist's touch, the immortal soul with the immutable psyche."[4]

Unfortunately, human nature is such that if one finds someone's position disagreeable, he or she will deem it inconsequential and even paint it maliciously as wanton or detrimental. This raises the question as to why, after all, the world cannot be on one wavelength, but that is also justifiable and evident. We have discontinuity, which people often confuse with the world being wholly incongruous.

---

[3] Nicholas G. Petryszak, "Tabula rasa–its origins and implications," *Journal of the History of the Behavioral Sciences* 17, no. 1 (January 1981): 15-2727.

[4] Richard Thompson Ford, *Dress Codes: How the Laws of Fashion Made History* (New York: Simon & Schuster, 2021), 43.

Us in the Digital Age

In this digital age, ample questions about technology and its effects are posed every day. The effects are rife and ripe. One of the main issues is the idea that technology has either enhanced or impeded human progress, overall advancement (through creativity and therapy), therapy itself, and creativity itself. We also are reminded that communication has gone from wholesome face-to-face interactions to virtual, impersonal interactions. We tend to collectively justify that face-to-face interactions are archaic. The truth is they are indispensable. We need them in this age, as we always have. They are deeply rooted in us and in our societies.

We have serious threats, like hacking and phishing. I see my Facebook friends posting statuses saying that they were hacked. We also have an evolutionary, progressive system by which we can access information, ideals, ideas, and arts. There is a distinguishable diversity and variety in information and information literacy now; it is increasingly convenient and globalized. We share ideas with one another at tremendous speeds, unimaginable to people in the past. We are in the digital age, or information age, when our ancestors were once in the stone age.

Sense of Self

I acknowledge here that I am narrowing the field considerably from the overarching human condition to a sense of self we all need to harness. We all naturally have it, and it is surprisingly easy to harbor and harness. Creativity is ultimately transcendent and helps us go beyond a sense of self. Before this journey (of creativity), it is important to establish a resolute and consolidated sense of self. (I recognize that the point I bring forward is that we are intrinsically creative beings. However, I want to say creativity is automatically in us. We still need to practice strategies to harness it wholly.)

Creativity and being innovative is revealing. It can work wonders. This may sound like a fable, but maybe it is fair to say creativity is dreamlike; it helps us achieve, accomplish, and enact things we never expected to do and pathways we never imagined. I know that is a weighty statement, but it could be true. I qualify the statement because not everyone equally harnesses the sense of self. Some people face barriers to unlocking the full creativity that correlates with action. Creativity is theory and action but it has to be enacted; it must.

Autonomy versus Independence

I have always thought of autonomy more as an adventure and independence as a mind state. You have autonomy; you don't possess independence. Autonomy is more of an action word where independence is more about proximity (or apparent lack thereof.) Independence is often portrayed in a positive light, but those who are described as independent can be seen as loners. This is not true. Loners, incidentally, are not losers, as society claims sometimes. I had to qualify that statement, because we all tend to look at independence a little differently.

Someone who is independent, by its very definition, does not depend on others. However, that does not make him or her a reclusive person or a misanthrope in any way. I know that seems absolutist to say and that my chosen terms are extreme, but is it not true? When someone is not married by a certain age, many societies grow skeptical, maybe even cynical. They ask, "Why is this person not married?"

We need both independence and autonomy. Autonomy refers to the aforementioned sense of self. Autonomy is liberating and leads to independence. Yes, they are different terms, but they are corollaries. Independence, once we debunk the myths and preconceptions of it, is a state of mind that is perpetual and elucidating. When we are independent, our eyes literally and figuratively open to a generally less lethargic, more open, and active life. We should practice both, and we should be mindful that they do not necessarily have set constraints. We can, however, have parameters for them.

Labels: Our Branding

I don't want to frame this as favoring labels, but I do not want to be automatically dismissive of labels either. Let us think out loud and assess this concept together. Labels are usually given a negative connotation; to my recollection, they are not brought up as abundantly as other things. Labels simplify the world in a way that is reductive and oversimplistic. Labels make us part of a community, but not in the ideal manner. Labels can put us in an in group as opposed to an out group. They provide a sense of belonging, which is a part of self-actualization. We need these both, according to Abraham Maslow.[5] I still haven't given my verdict, but readers can clearly see I am not a fan of their complicity in making the world too simple. Simplicity leaves out an individual's traits and defining features; that should not be the case.

I am not saying anonymity is better; maybe in some cases it is. It is a privilege for someone to get to know another person's story. It is a good idea to keep certain ideals inside. I cite the reasoning one will usually resort to: the idea of trust. When we cannot trust a person we just met, we know we should not overshare. Anonymity masks us. It makes us blend into the crowd while taking away our identities. Labels may do that too. They put us into groups while taking away other attributes we would like to be defined by.

My verdict is that labels and anonymity are neither good nor bad; they are neutral but not innocuous. We should be careful when using them or bestowing them upon others. They should be considered in moderation.

---

[5] Abraham Maslow and K. J. Lewis. "Maslow's Hierarchy of Needs." *Salenger Incorporated* 14, no. 17 (1987): 987–990.

Therapy: A Domino Effect

Therapy is so many things—positive, evolutionary, revolutionary things—other than just therapy. It helps you turn your life around; it has a way of its own—one I cannot even fully decipher. In therapy, you have a pragmatic, programmatic system. It operates and functions in a way that personalizes the client. The client will feel less robotic and pay attention to his or her actions and thoughts more. The way it works is also a domino effect, a chain reaction. Once someone receives therapy, he or she feels adequate and wants to pass it on. The person pays it forward. The client is a healthier person and a more operational, functional being who can be a constructive and decisive influence on other people's lives. After all, life is vast; life is intricate—we need someone if not more than one person—as we ruminate on the term "self-sufficient."

I would add smiling to the category of contagious actions that are therapeutic or have the potential to improve one's mood. Smiles are simple acts of kindness; they are infectious. As the cliché goes, "Laughter is the best medicine." You smile when you laugh. No matter how genuine your smile is, you are trying, and most people will see your effort. The effort is what goes a long way.

Thinking Figuratively

In English classes in grade school, my fellow students would agonize when we studied symbols. Symbolism came to me naturally, and I was able to think in a symbolic, allegorical way. In other words, I was able to lend insight to what an item meant or represented when others thought it meaningless and/or arbitrary.

I am happy to announce that it is not actually difficult or agonizing to think symbolically or allegorically. Let us first start with symbols. I want to go beyond my English class story and tell readers that symbols may not always form a coherent narrative; however, they are omnipresent. I do not think that they are ubiquitous only to an extent. In my opinion, they *are* everywhere, *all of the time*. They carry properties, like being inanimate objects or animate like animals or friends. Your friends can be your symbols but also your allegories. The stories of how you met your friends can be allegorized by those bonds.

What I aim for by talking about allegory here is the concept that everything has a story behind it. I know some people, maybe animists, believe that everything has a spirit. I remember how in the song "Colors of the Wind" from the Disney film *Pocahontas*, Pocahontas suggests that everything has a spirit and a name.[6]

Thinking figuratively, or thinking in literary devices like hyperbole, synecdoche, and others is often a beneficial way to shift perspectives.

The Curious Status Quo

Status quo is a term that has gained popularity in the past, probably because it is understood more. Is it understood as negative or positive? That is my question. I want to say the status quo itself in an innocuous thing. It is just that way things are, by definition. The status quo manifests culturally, and thus we want to confront it. The status quo can be synonymous with tradition—the way things are and *have been*. The status quo causes us to be unstable and jittery—it triggers us. It makes us uncomfortable with how things are, and change is always welcome. It is or becomes reality—disembodied and untouchable—but is also undesirable. It hides our *agency*. We cannot function fully without this agency. We cannot functionally make free choices. Our existence become somewhat arbitrary, but the forward-facing fact is that we can change the status quo—even if it is painstakingly gradual.

Our ability to make meaning is inherently threatened. The meaning gets stifled into existing in a vacuum. The meaning is

---

[6] Mike Gabriel and Eric Goldberg, *Pocahontas*, (1995; Burbank, CA: Buena Vista Pictures, 2000), DVD.

skewed to a traditional, cultural standpoint and worldview. We need to make meaning of the world in order to function as wary individuals or groups. Meaning making processes can also be freed from the status quo, and we can think critically to make these meanings.

Are you brave enough to challenge the status quo or system? It is already fragmented and dysfunctional, and it is susceptible to its own demise, so why are you afraid or hesitant or apprehensive? The clock is ticking and thoughts and questions flood your mind. *How long is forever? Will time heal everything?* What I can say for sure is not an answer but a response: time will wait for nobody. Time and the world is yours to an extent; avail yourselves of it.

I acknowledge that it can be daunting to challenge the status quo and change it, because it is quite rooted. Sometimes, what seems imperceptible to grapple with and virtually impossible to confront is what needs to be confronted. We need to change the status quo in general, in this vast landscape of hate and toxicity. What I mean is to be more inquisitive, observant, and consequently more proactive about the condition.

Frames and Threads

Information (or thoughts or what have you) is naturally framed; it is always framed in a certain way with a certain agenda. In her 2001 TED Talk, Tina Seelig mentions how creativity arises from how ideas are framed. She talks about how questions are framed determined by this.[7] You should pay close attention to how you frame your thoughts. This is extremely predictive and indicative of how you come across in your communications and how they are returned. The way questions are framed when presented to you determines how you answer them or what is elicited or evoked by them.

If you haven't figured it out yet, I am borrowing the terms from literature. Frames and threads dictate the direction, diction, and conviction of a story or narrative. They contextualize the story by

---

[7] Seelig, "Crash Course Creativity," 18:15.

setting the scene with space, place, mood, tone, and so on. It is the same in life. Each of us is on a journey. This journey may be ubiquitous in the sense that it is embarked on and felt by everyone, but it is different for everyone. With that being said, the thread, *which in this case I define as perspective or point of view,* will always be different. It has different ramifications and iterations of meaning in a person's life and his or her agency to make decisions. The past and future frame the present, sometimes by being the context of the present and having influencing factors. The past, especially, provides a thread with which to look at life. Futures are more uncertain—not in a bad way, but they are more disembodied. They have to be seen in foresight, as the past is more concrete and is factual rather than projected.

In another sense, frames are moods controlling other moods. Moods frame undertones of reactions that lead to consequences; this is a process. The reactions elicited by a situation or condition in your life certainly have consequences and ramifications that instill moods. This process becomes institutionalized in you and also rooted in you. You become accustomed to the fact that one mood (the way it is framed) makes another mood instantly foreseeable and/or inevitable.

Comfort Zones

Comfort zones are generally viewed in a favorable way. They carry positive connotations, but are also being increasingly recognized for their double-sided nature. Like Lee Cockerell says in the episode "You've Got to Know More to Be More" of the podcast *Creating Disney Magic,* stepping out of your comfort zones and doing things that make you uncomfortable are things you need to try; they also make you grow and be more reflective. You "develop a personality taking risks," Cockerell says. He also says the process is "progressive."

In the end, taking risks is generally the advantageous way in which you can broaden perspectives and think more critically and widely. [8]

Points of View

Everyone has a different way of looking at the world and the animate and inanimate things that reside in it. Some people have a more bleak, pessimistic point of view and some a more positive, forward-thinking point of view. Either way, our points of view are shaped by our experiences.

When I recently re-watched the first six films of the *Star Wars* franchise, I realized there are so many insightful and profound sayings that speak to point of view. In *Star Wars Episode II: Attack of the Clones*, Palpatine tells Anakin Skywalker that good is a point of view. [9] In *Star Wars Episode VI: The Return of the Jedi*, the spirit of Obi-Wan Kenobi tells Luke Skywalker that the narrative that Darth Vader killed Luke's father and also betrayed Luke's father is a point of view. [10]

Media Is a Medium (Good or Bad?)

As you can see, there's a question—a thought-provoking, ongoing, painstaking question—in the title of this section. Is media good or bad? In this book, it is perhaps more bad than good. This is morbid and decrepit, but is it not true? The media is a medium for creativity, but it is still limited and limiting. That it is not to say it is useless. Maybe I am being too harsh and crude. The media does have some

---

[8] Lee Cockerell and Jody Mayberry, "You've Got to Know More to Be More," *Creating Disney Magic*, podcast audio, July 2021, https://open.spotify.com/show/6ThERLxDTQlf16TBNyVPPS.
[9] George Lucas, *Star Wars Episode II: Attack of the Clones*, (1999; Los Angeles, CA: 20th Century Fox, 2002), DVD.
[10] Richard Marquand, *Star Wars Episode VI: The Return of the Jedi*, (1983; Los Angeles, CA: 20th Century Fox, 2005), DVD.

uplifting and beneficial aspects. It is an outlet that, if used correctly, can portray the maligned in a positive manner. Maybe it is not *inherently* bad, but it has to be utilized correctly and *accurately*.

The baffling concept that the media *is, in fact,* a double-edged sword implies that it is sharp. It can do damage to the positive or negative. It can be useful but also too useful. This means that it can be used for the wrong reasons and in the wrong ways. This, unfortunately, is usually the case. I was a proponent of media but studying it made me more neutral. Sure, there media is everywhere. It manifests as expression and inclusion, but to restate a cliché, "too much of a good thing is a bad thing." That is my verdict about *media*.

The media, for one, tends to be partial and polarized; maybe that is why we get the *partial* picture of life. Undoubtedly, it shapes our worldviews. Being a liberal, I have noticed that CNN caters to me, but it does not cater to the other side. It creates an *echo chamber*, continuously reinforcing and reaffirming the view of one side, painting the other side as virtually insignificant or even nonexistent. The problem with echo chambers is that they make us accustomed to myopia and agreement, which is not how the world works. Our views will not always be reaffirmed or resonated with, and we need to be wary of this. The positive facet of this is we can be open to embracing all kinds of views, even when we do not agree. We can agree to disagree, and sometimes this is the best course of action. It pacifies necessary moments.

We are bombarded with melancholy stories, so we lose hope and think of the world as a helplessly selfish, downtrodden, and inhumane place. The good part is that is not true. It is *not* the way a person should shape his or her perspective. The news constantly overwhelms viewers with sad stories and throws in a few feel-good stories that undoubtedly lift spirits but do not compensate.

For example, on *ABC World News Tonight*, I have noticed that first viewers watch school shootings, oil spills, killings, COVID (which is to be taken *seriously* and not lightly, by the way), unruly airline passengers, and even cruise ship passengers falling overboard. Then there are the "America Strong" or "Made in America" segments;

while these stories do elate me a bit, I have just been barraged with sad, depressing stories.

The media, additionally, has a facet of confirmation bias and the availability bias/heuristic. What is most accessible and comprehensible becomes easiest to internalize. We institutionalize it, which can be good or bad, depending on whether its implementation and realization is good or bad. When views confirm us, validate us, and align with our views, we find them to be closer to us in proximity and in agreement. The positive facet of this goes with the saying "great minds think alike." When two or more genuinely great minds think alike, we all benefit when their idea gains traction. Media leads to word-of-mouth as the information trickles down to masses of people; thus it is the ultimate source of push and pull for movements or thoughts.

Reactionary Things

We, as humans, are inherently reactionary. We are not robotic in this sense. We are triggered by certain things and react without fail. We can react impulsively or in a premeditated manner. Either way, it is almost reiterative to the idea that every action has a reaction. I find this to be inarguably true. Even if we do not react aggressively or impetuously, the impulse may build in us. We may have been abused and respond in kind to others. We can engage in reactive "anything." This is important to note.

We must realize we are flawed as humans and that we need to be kept in check. We need to think that being infinitely capable is a true double-edged sword. While we can reaffirm ourselves and ascertain our limitlessness repeatedly, we can also see that we are capable of doing *bad* things. I know this sounds morbid, but with constant reminders, we can conquer this. Everyone, in this case, has a bad side.

Push and Pull

I want to point out how the world is composed of push and pull. It is present everywhere and constitutes most situations; perhaps this is exemplified by yin and yang and roughly by the color wheel. The color wheel shows opposites and the yin and yang is composed of opposites as well. We thus witness and attest that there are evident tensions in the world. They sometimes cause friction and even (maybe a bit more rarely) consensus. Thus, it is indispensable and necessary to acknowledge the push and pull of things.

In art, I want to give an abundantly clear example. Art has many themes in all of its mediums and forms. In a vast, overarching sense, art constitutes dichotomies of many sorts and thus has a natural push and pull. This is depicted by conflicting themes and motifs, like nature or water. It is most obvious when we talk about color. When warm and cool hues blend or conflict, this tension or interaction makes its presence known.

Social Comparisons and Social Mobility

There are upward and downward social comparisons, and it is easy to tell which is beneficial and which is disadvantageous. In many cultural and ethnic communities, like my own, parents count friends' children as successful and look down upon their own children. This is toxic to the psyche of a person, no matter how old. It can have benign to severe effects. It can certainly cause a person to doubt himself or herself in myriad ways—a scenario that even typing about devastates me. I can empathize because I have experienced these comparisons, which, fortunately, do not occur anymore. Downward comparisons (when you compare yourself to a person of lower status than you) are positive; you will look at yourself more positively. Upward comparisons should be avoided at all costs. They leave lasting imprints and cause self-sabotage by making us feel inadequate. Unfortunately, these have become mainstays; they are incredibly pervasive and accessible to a person. Upward comparisons can take the form of comparing yourself to a celebrity or influencer. These will always make you look down upon yourself. The celebrity or influencer will be projecting a considerably more privileged life.

We usually use relative language when we make comparisons. We might feel like we are being prejudiced, presumptuous, judgmental, or even biased when using such language. That is a barrage of negative words, but does that mean we avoid using relative language? The truth is that we cannot avoid it. It is interwoven into society and language as it is. Can we mask it? We should just be cautious when using such language, not to come off as hierarchical or disparaging. We can do this by:

1. Controlling what we compare;
2. Controlling who we are comparing;
3. Being vigilant about the diction we use (and not sounding condescending or patronizing); and
4. Remembering we are all human and no one is above anyone except in obvious situations (e.g., having an advantage in the job market when you have more experience related to the job or having the title of PhD as opposed to a lower degree; remember that educated people are not even necessarily more enlightened in certain aspects).

By not being judgmental or using such language, we can foster a healthy and nurturing culture. A nurturing culture is one in which relationships and support from those relationships contribute to success or act as goals.[11]

We often use Venn diagrams to compare. We subconsciously use juxtaposition. We put ourselves side by side with groups or individuals and compare and contrast based on intelligence, confidence, looks, likeability, popularity, and other factors. We make social and cultural comparisons that can motivate us and daunt us.

---

[11] Ronald Alder, Lawrence Rosenfeld, & Russel Proctor II. *Interplay* (New York, NY: Oxford University Press, 2010), 49.

The simple fix is what I mentioned earlier: to always use downward social comparisons. These sound like you are looking downward, and this is true. They sound paradoxical though, and they might be. In any case, make these judgments with caution. Remember to not let these comparisons make you overzealous, daunt you, or make you feel like you lack something. They can even make you lackadaisical, but always remember there is a better you waiting to be discovered. With every step in the present, you are the most perfect form of you that you can be.

Assumptions

Assumption, as a word, has a neutral connotation, but I am here to paint it with a moreover negative connotation. Assumptions can be good, though, when we infer something from our context. They can aid us in navigating the world and can feel like cushioned when we need to be cushioned. Other than that, being presumptuous, which I personally conflate with assumptions, is potentially damaging. It is inhibiting in the sense that it prohibits us from seeing what we have set ourselves against seeing. We selectively see and see what we want to believe; this is human nature.

Reaffirmation and Potential

In order to unlock a reaffirming potential (that is not an uncertain one), we must do a few things. We must exorcise the negativity—this involves woeful and impetuous self-talk. We must also debunk banal and overdone myths. One example is how people are constantly imprinted with the cliché and tediously discouraging belief that money is security—the only security. This leads (however indirectly but not inadvertently) to anthropomorphizing creativity. This intertwines and connects the spirit or soul to mind to body. We are all three interlaced beautifully by these three essentially and symbiotically complementing one another. When one is affected, the other two are thusly affected.

Reaffirmations can be highly spiritual. In my experience, I have also had them reinforced by my actions. For example, when I write a new poem or learn a new word, I am reaffirmed of my literary capacities (even as I write this book).

Before moving to the next section, I want to highlight how curious I became after realizing reaffirmation (to an extent) can be a double-edged sword. It can be too self-ascertaining at times when echoed by myriad sources, thus becoming a problematic echo chamber. Let us carefully consider affirmation to be comprehensive, circumspect, and impartial. Affirmations are in no way unhealthy, and it feels awfully strange to consider that there is a negative side to them. However, let us be rational and remember the cliché that maybe even here "too much of a good thing is a bad thing." Echo chambers are not just problematic, but they can have numerous damaging effects. They can cause one to have a small-minded approach to typical and mundane ideas and a myopic, sheltered view of the world.

Affirmations, which do sometimes lead to echo chambers, cann have two effects that oppose one another. In one way, it makes someone more susceptible to adopt a perpetual victim mentality. We know it is extremely unhealthy to constantly be given a victim role and also for one to be accustomed to such a role. The victim mentality requires no self-accountability. The other side of this is the complete and evident opposite. The person will self-incriminate—this is just my ideal. The person will *only* do this if the reaffirmations cause guilt. That is entirely dependent on the person in question. If he or she self-deprecates, it is because he or she feels responsible. Again, that is a *good thing* and too much of it is a *bad thing*. The person is praised so much or re-ascertained by others to a point where compliments make them stalwart and afraid. They feel the pressure of dire and fraught expectations. They will not blame others by using victim mentality, as in the other case, but will profusely feel dreadful guilt and blame themselves.

Echo chambers reinforce confirmation bias and dependency on it. One will tend to become accustomed to what is favorable to hear or witness for himself or herself. Echo chambers can limit and inhibit us from seeing farther and gazing into another's crucial perspective. We can bounce ideas off another person's perspective and insights; we can feed off them and shape our perspectives more comprehensively.

Structure versus Direction

Life often lacks structure and can lack direction. These are both dire and essential to life; feeling deprived of them can cause instability. Structure and direction are consistent with each other and carry similar thematic meanings and connotations. They can be entangled with one another and confused with one another.

Structure is needed in life to navigate it. Having structure, to me, means everything is falling into place like a jigsaw puzzle. Direction is different because, essentially, it occupies a different part of life. Direction calls to the future. Structure calls on us to mend the present, whereas direction sets up for the future. Direction is felt when we can *foresee* our futures. Structure is when we can trust our surroundings in the present.

Security or Sanity?

Security is essentially synonymous with sanity. They complement and feed into each other. Navigating this composite life is a conundrum, filled with disruptive mistakes and elevating decisions and victories. To embark on these victories, security is key. It will be present in the positive outcomes in life. Security is directly related to sanity. One cannot exist without the other. This makes the two synonymous and consistent with each other. Furthermore, security and sanity do not just co-exist; they are indispensable to each other as corollaries. When you're secure, you're sane. When you're sane, you're secure.

Material Things

Material things are deceptive and illusory. I know they are omnipresent, so it makes little sense to be this morbid about them. Reflectively speaking, however, they are. Of course, material is material and reminds us of the term materialistic. Material things can also conflate with satisfying and satiating feelings, but they can be elusive and cause detachment (ironically) from an entwined world.

In an inescapably, axiomatically commodified world, we often see that our feelings can be advertised. To put it colloquially, our feelings are "put on blast." This can cause avoidance rather than the positive facet of identification. When we look at this critical side of material and commodities, we see that the increasing tendencies of people to commodify emotions is strategic and cumbersome. For example, unrequited love or failure are often reinforced in ads promoting Valentine's Day or being a doctor or engineer. On the bright side, ads also inspire unity and depolarize us. They are aspirational in nature and overall healthy and positive. I have seen ads for Dove inspiring diversity, and it is not only Dove. The fashion industry is facing constant criticism for its cultural appropriation and racial issues (sometimes blatant racism or then discrimination). As a result, it is making efforts to curb this criticism through initiatives of representation, even in body positivity (or body neutrality.) I often see that we are perpetuating the rhetoric "not tested on animals." We also see healthy ads for coming together. In California, we have ads for California medical centers stating "Hello humankindness." The classic "Got milk?" campaign is everywhere. Positive ads discouraging vaping or inspiring people to get COVID vaccines are also necessitated by a polarized country and atmosphere. We also have ads for Pass It On that extol different virtues. They inspire our states of mind to be more resolute and stable. They make us feel union, camaraderie, and urgency where needed.

Voids

The presence of a void is one that induces unnamable, immeasurable anxiety. Having a void that needs to be filled is vexing; it is bothersome and reappears constantly in life. Human nature renders us naturally devoid—in our minds—even when we are not deprived of anything we actually need. Of course, this is not to downplay the fact that self-actualization, as per Abraham Maslow's hierarchy of needs, is a serious, nonnegotiable, and imperative need. This is what I want to refer to with voids, because this one is underestimated. Fill the voids within you when you begin your journey. This will be recurrent, but it has to be taken care of. Usually, if your void is intangible and abstract, it will not be too inconvenient to fulfill it. I usually write a poem or read or jot down a thought. This has proven to be beneficial to me.

Power of the Written Word

We must also conquer and understand the power of the written word, which is more concrete (but not necessarily more monolithic) than the spoken word. The creative written word has a definite but infinite power that can be—and frankly must be—harnessed in so many ways. That we must unveil that creativity is not just formulaic; we have to paint with it (no pun intended) but we can paint with literal paint or with flowing words. We will paint mosaics that speak to us.

The written word is presented to you and by you; it is a mutual, reciprocal phenomenon and dialectic. It enriches you as you enrich it. The written word has much to offer you as you have much to offer to it. It takes on myriad forms and lives in molds galore. It can be poetry, creative nonfiction, prose, prose poetry, onomatopoeia, synecdoche, metonymy, metaphor, personification, simile, allegory, and so on.

Communication in Therapy

It is also important to remember that artistic and creative pursuits can erode and transcend anxiety and toxicity. The art culture takes precedence naturally over the toxic culture in societies. Therapy and communication are corollaries. They inextricably, by default, go together. Interpersonal communication is indispensable to therapy as is inter-gender and intercultural communication. All of this blends together to mirror and facilitate therapy. Therapy is a discourse—a productive, transformative, and purposeful one. It is a conversation, and it *is* communication. It is dialogue—two-way, invested dialogue—and involves not just talking but also actively listening, prodding, and prompting for more dialogue.

As therapy is communication, principles apply similarly. Therapy is thus relational and multidirectional. Therapy *is* based on a system of exchange, since it hinges on both the practitioner/therapist and patient/client being candid and open. It is then intercultural and inter-gender, which means it has the dynamics and intricacies respective of all of its characteristics. Interpersonal communication is interdependent. It involves as many participants in the said communication (or in this case, therapy) as possible.

Our language can waver on a spectrum from specific to abstract, and conversely as well. For this concept, I would like to invoke the abstraction ladder, probably most prominently used in interpersonal communication.[12] The shift from concrete to abstract can make things more vague, ambivalent, and/or ambiguous. Despite this, this represents a shift to a more meaningful, emotional type of language, rather than a targeted way of communicating. When someone's language is concrete, it also can be targeting, blaming, or scapegoating. On the other hand, specific language cites examples and is not anecdotal. Anecdotal language calls attention to feelings, opinions, and perception, while concrete language is empiricist and can be statistical. This does not, however, mean that specific

---

[12] Adler, Rosenfeld, & Proctor II, 155.

language encompasses more or is more impactful in a person's life. In my humble opinion, it may be true that concrete language is more factually rooted since it can be more readily supported by evidence.

We converge, or assimilate, in language and its mannerisms to match the individuals or groups with whom we are in contact.[13]

Just like in a therapy group, you must remember to articulate and cohere your thoughts when speaking, creating and fostering an open yet intimate communication climate in the group. This involves verbal and nonverbal language and exists on a spectrum. It moves back and forth dynamically. Nonverbal cues, like facial expressions, are just as crucial as verbal cues. The example I think of is my therapist seeing me and saying I look happy or content. This creates the atmosphere as well, as she then prompts me to delve into my feelings and thoughts. Looking alert and interested is a must in therapy; it is important to let your clients know you care—that is a no-brainer. As a client, you must also engage, giving the therapist talking points and content to decipher and deal with.

Therapy is relational. In its very pursuit, as I have said before, it *is* communication and it has interpersonal and intrapersonal aspects. Therapy is relational because it involves the reciprocation of articulated sentiments from both sides (more so from the client), sympathy from the therapist, and candor on both sides (though it may be more of a responsibility for the client). It requires a level of understanding, a common ground being met by both sides. I want to highlight how ubiquitous commonalities or common ground have become (fortunately) in our world. It has and permeated realms of fiction and non-fiction. Jack Duquesne, in the TV series *Hawkeye*, says that "common interest is very fertile ground for bonding."[14]

For example, therapy will be much more conveniently mediated and facilitated if both sides agree on many issues. A more conservative (in whatever way) therapist and a liberal client may not see eye to eye;

---

[13] Adler, Rosenfeld, & Proctor II, 147.

[14] *Hawkeye*. 2021. Season 1 Episode 2. "Hide and Seek." Directed by Rhys Thomas. Aired on November 24, 2021 on Disney Plus. https://www.disneyplus.com/video/79f8992c-82b6-41d8-bf5e-b25b94966561.

even if both sides try to ignore this, it will appear as an issue in the way the conversation of therapy is carried out. Everyone in my life knows of my keen knowledge of Disney and investment in it, so I expect them to bear with me and add to the conversation when I talk. Some people passively listen, and I appreciate that immensely, while I do appreciate feedback and prompting from others. Prompting is when the other person (or people) prompt or prod you on to keep speaking about the topic at hand.

This can be nonverbal, with facial expressions or head nods. These are essentially the nonverbal cues. It is vital to notice nonverbal cues. They speak volumes (to restate a cliché). They are so trite and subtle that they must be emphasized and are often overlooked. A flirty playing with the hair (manipulation) or nodding (to let someone know you are listening and want to hear more) are indispensable. The fact that many scholars have been able to construct salient theories (a few of which I invoked for my master's thesis project) on nonverbal communication means something. I invoked expectancy violations theory—in that case the nonverbal expectations and cues given by the media and by some Muslims—which can explain expectations of a haggard, haphazard person. The person could be empathetic and intelligible and will be misjudged. That is why it is imperative to pay meticulous attention to nonverbals that are omnipresent.

Listening is, as Lee Cockerell says in "How to Be a Better Listener," an episode of his podcast *Creating Disney Magic*, one of our five senses.[15] It is undoubtedly one of the most important for communication. Vision is also important to see how far you can envision dreams and/or aspirations, but also to communicate visually and vividly. It is important to not just listen actively by prompting, prodding, and probing at the right tempo, but to listen proactively and validate the other person's musings, utterances, and thoughts. It is really an art. Listening can create pathways to trust; *not* listening

[15] Lee Cockerell and Jody Mayberry, "How to Be a Better Listener," *Creating Disney Magic*, podcast audio, August 2021, https://open.spotify.com/episode/1awnQSBb9QmVtFBhkIhYeW.

can create room and possibility for poor decisions. It can also create voids and tensions if not done right.

Furthermore, we cannot be technical in our language in therapy or creativity, mainly because we want to convey deep, profound insight and heartfelt, authentic emotion. Technical language is undesirable here, as it is neutral and does not produce or suggest anything in the realms we are concerned with in therapy or in the creative world.

A therapy session can have the client using solid, concrete examples to exemplify his or her situation, or it can take the shape of narration, where the person provides stories and experiences from his or her life. These are descriptive and anecdotal. The system of dialogue therapy can take can be classified as cause and effect. It is not always employed. Generically, a person wants to take accountability or blame the obvious culprit (no matter if it is a person or an abstract thing.)

Open communication is indispensable. One must be honest, but even more importantly, transparent. It is a reciprocal phenomenon because it produces and necessitates dialogue. Workplace communication highlights this as do personal relationships.

Finally, let's assess what failure to communicate really does. Its magnitude and effects are catastrophic, when projected. Failure to communicate is what has caused calamities and voids to exist. It has created gaps and commotion, discombobulating us, and disrupting coherency between nations, groups, business entities, celebrities, and the public, among others. Making an effort to communicate often cannot go wrong; it is rewarding. It goes a long way. Effectively and efficiently equipping ourselves with communication amends the flow of conversation, keeps it constant, and prevents culmination or breakage of relationships.

Connotations and Denotations

In creative realms and in therapy, we must acknowledge that diction and conviction are both generally and relatively more anecdotal. Words are exponentially more connotative than denotative. Feeling, insight, and perception is evoked more than set information. Of course, that is not to rule out that denotative language exists in creative conversations and in therapy.

For example, factual information and words will inevitably be employed but the context will vary and feelings will still be evoked, provoked, and invoked. Denotative words will have a less characteristic, more impersonal feel than connotative words. An example is "casualty" versus "hurt"; hurt is a word that indicates various types of pain and casualty cannot be more or less than injury.

Individuality, Subjectivity, and Positionality

Before I continue into other facets of the mind, I want to shed light on accountability. This is something important for us all to have. Accountability means to own up to our status as humans—flawed ones. We are all flawed, and our flaws arguably determine who we are; they are characteristics of us. Similarly, we must be responsible people. We are to be responsible for our thoughts and actions to a specified extent and standard (one that cannot vary; that would be unfair). We must not be toxic, as I will elaborate, and we must not adopt victim mentality. This weakens us, but not only us. It weakens others and connections to others thus weakening our networks, making them more linear and less beneficial to us. In the end, we must suffer. The less we blame others or other factors, the less we adopt a victim mentality, and the less we will ultimately regret and suffer. We will still take responsibility for our deeds.

Being creative is dutiful, and it preoccupies us. Just like we have a resonating, weighted responsibility to be creative, we also have to have accountability for ourselves. When we inhabit accountability and manifest it in our lives, we become infinite—transcendent as humans and sensible as beings.

Lexicons of Creativity

Lexicons of creativity should be idiomatic and subliminal, but telling, subtle, and approachable. They are inherent in a language that is naturally codified. Unpacking that language should be sublime and able to be done—i.e., it should be accessible. I believe creativity is meant to be complex and intricate but also decipherable and able to be broken down. When it becomes convoluted, it becomes sequestered and stifling. That is why I call, incidentally, for a universal reading of creative forms and mediums. Achieving this is a long and collectivistic road and one I eagerly suggest we embark on.

Some words or terms can be binarized. One of these duos is mutual and reciprocal. A mutual communication is called for inherently by therapy and by living therapeutically. One cannot live on a one-way street, so to speak, to heal and grow. A person must be given what he or she gives, reciprocally. That means it whatever the person gives is returned. If it is mutual (which is idyllic but maybe often utopian) it is reciprocated in the exact and equal amounts.

Language (which may be used rather synonymously with lexicons), according to Noam Chomsky is his book, *Reflections on Language*, is both inborn and follows a system. Language and learning influence each other, as I would further his arguments. They do this because they both are universally used. They are both everyday phenomena; you use language every day and typically learn something new, perhaps novel, to you. With that said, in therapy and in creativity, language is weighed. It is, according to Chomsky, informed by other structures in the mind.[16] I would further this by specifying that psyche, disposition or temperament, and environment influence self-talk, language in therapy, and the disembodied language we subconsciously make use of when we are getting those "creative juices flowing."

---

[16] Noam Chomsky, *On Language* (Cambridge, MA: Temple Smith, 1976), 41.

Codes

We live in an encoded world dictated by symbols, and yes, codes. Race, religion, culture, and institutions all impose and enforce such codes. Codes are not always negative but are often overlooked. Some, like school, follow a developmental and progressing pattern.

Vulnerability

Vulnerability has quite the negative connotation. Is it a controversial word? Let's just say I think so. In order to authentically and honestly confront certain notions and phrases, we should recontextualize their negative connotations. This will also aid us in expanding our worldviews and horizons. Vulnerability might imply or connote weakness or apprehensiveness. While this is not wrong, it is not resolute. What I mean is that it has other, more positive connotations. In realms of therapy, this word is encouraged and commended. It is the backbone to the person. Recontextualizing is a skill; it is not a talent. It reminds me of an excerpt from my favorite classic television show, *Friends*. It is from an episode where a finger is found in food that Monica prepared. Her mother, who is often extremely critical of her, said she "pulled a Monica." Near the end of the episode, Phoebe tells her to try again and be successful and, thus, recontextualize "pulling a Monica."[17]

Vulnerability, and its image as a word/term, it is a cathartic way to release feelings; it is an effective outlet. It takes ample forms and serve myriad purposes. You can even say vulnerability is putting thoughts on paper. This is one of its forms. This is not intrinsically negative, as you can see, so in pointing out this form of it, I am also providing a positive image of it.

---

[17] *Friends*. 1997. Season 4 Episode 3, "The One with the Cuffs." Directed by Pete Bonerz. Aired October 9, 1997 on KTLA.

How does one reflect vulnerability? How can one be willing or made willing to reflect vulnerability (which incidentally and probably may utmost reflect weakness)?

Stigmatization

You can easily and innovatively utilize creativity to combat stigmas, which is one of its many uses. You can confront other problems with it, but stigmas reflect toxicity in society. They define people and impede them from being their authentic selves. It is self-defeating, since it does not serve any purpose. It breaches and impedes rudimentary and innate creativity in many capacities. It is unfortunately so prevalent that it is even intangible and invisible—to a point where it becomes elusive to confront. It is derisive and illusory, but must be stopped. It is universal, so to stop it is a feat—not a daunting feat though.

Some examples of stigmas can be given, but the list would be exhaustive. Stigmas can control our perceptions of the world. Stigmas make some things seem heterodox. In reality, they might be, but they take the beauty out of whatever it is at hand. Stigmas are virtually notional, conjectural. They are not real and are constructions. They are placed or imposed upon us to connote and shape our horizons. They may even control how far we positively and productively see into those horizons.

Ethics and Principles

The truth is that we are socialized into a reductionist, categorical, schematic world. We are exposed to a world where classifying beings and things into groups is made advantageous by societies, communities, and histories. With this, we practice etiquettes (some particular to our cultures or heritages), and we adopt mannerisms that are socially desirable. We act with ethics and avoid looking immoral. This is problematic because some acts are culturally codified and perceived as deviant, but they can be redefined and harm no one. They are categorized as harmful or disadvantageous acts, but they need recontextualizing. In cultural circles, these are particularly visible and eminent. I can point out so many ideals from my culture that are conflated with religion; people tend to view people who practice that religion or culture as backward. Some of these do seem backward and restrictive, maybe even archaic, yet in moderation, we see sense in them.

Examples are not cursing (which is not specific to my culture, religion, or heritage), dressing modestly (which pertains to my culture and religion), and not being too available to the opposite sex. We see these as, once again, regressive. When looked at in moderation, however, they can be considered on a cautious and circumspect basis and spectrum.

Now, I want to move on and discuss ethics and principles. Face-to-face communication is a phenomenon that is gaining traction as a lost art. Today, I would argue, it scarcely exists but is still important. The fact that it is continually dwindling frightens me. Face-to-face communication has advantages in many aspects and respects, like romantic and platonic relationships, or in the workplace.

Another controversial, widespread ethical dilemma is dress codes. Personally, I think they inadvertently make their followers anonymous by taking away expression and individuality and emphasizing the wrong ideals. I conjecture that, and propose that they are useless and ineffective, partly because most students, or others, would be reluctant to use them.

Cultural barriers feel daunting. They feel, and even might be, consolidated and unwavering. They feel like set precedents that were not set by the current times or people, which is why they become more obdurate and less fitting for an evolving world and its inhabitants.

Following principles can become problematic, and not following them seems liberating. They exist, though, for a reason and should be considered modestly or liberally.

Principles to Live By (Therapeutically)

I postulate some principles you will want to adopt and live by when in therapy. My argument is that we must always live therapeutically and live like we *are* in therapy at all times. Why should we?

We can feel better on so many levels and in so many capacities. To distinguish between the levels, we can use the terms *micro*, *meso*, and *macro*. We can do this (and I will go in-depth on it later on) through what I would call *mediums of therapy*, different forms of therapy or different platforms for it, in which one can find solace, escapism, catharsis, resolve, and so on.

Make sure you listen for or look for symbols in your journey. They sometimes are ubiquitous to us all and endemic, like a country's flag, or a color like green for jealousy. They can be personal or reminiscent of a generic concept or idea. The symbol can evoke many ideals and feelings.

For example, Disney symbolizes sheer euphoria for me. Disney parks are my happy places (Disneyland is the closest to me). They are physical manifestations and/or embodiments of Disney nerds (or Disney geeks, or whatever you want to call them) and their obsession or addiction to Disney. I am referring to total Disney geeks like me, but of course, Disney is nondiscriminatory and allows everyone; anyone can do Disney.

Generally, a few of the principles to live by (or thrive by, consequently) are these.

1. Frequency and consistency: You must continue a creative action that is helping you cope with a situation. You must be consistent with it and employ it frequently, so you are not falling into defeat.

2. Acceptance: When you are confronted with a certain situation, it is fruitless and useless to deny it. Reality has it that anything can happen; we must accept it and take action. Here, it is important for me to remind you that you must believe that only you can repair your situation; you

know it on a such an intimate level that is unique to you. This is empowering once you realize you are equipped, or can be equipped, to deal with the adversity that befalls you. You are your hero.

What Are The Mediums of Therapy?

First, these can be intrapersonal (to yourself) and interpersonal (social and communicative.) You can find therapy by yourself and by being around others. Try not to isolate yourself into a reclusive slump. I am a people person, so I adhere to this regularly. I talk to as many people I can per day and have no issue with it. Let's not forget anxiety—that elusive but deadly anxiety. I want to list the mediums of therapy after this brief introduction.

1) Popular culture encompasses not only physical entertainment or acts of it, but the trends and notions that trickle down from it. All of the names of celebrities and influencers— Viners (in the past), and today's TikTokers and YouTubers— are parts of popular culture. They have effectively seeped into multiple realms and everyday conversation.

2) Newspapers are virtually archaic today. They are reminiscent of old but could also resonate vintage. There is probably a charm in picking up a newspaper and reading it. Of course, there are two sides. There are people who prefer the tactile, traditional medium of newspapers and those who prefer online news. Of course, online news manifests itself in many ways. Let's focus on online newspapers and go into a newspaper chapter in which we discuss the advantages and disadvantages.

3) Magazines are part of the image of journalism that is being overtaken by the digital age. There are numerous advantages and disadvantages of print magazines and online magazines. Both can build communities around them but in different

ways with differing tactics. This is a conversation for the chapter on magazines.

4)   Television is a medium that is widely accessible (even though it is imperative to note that not all households—even in the United States—have televisions.) Television shows can be spinoffs of movies or of other television shows. *Joey* was a spinoff of my absolute favorite classic television show *Friends*. The latest example I can think of (of which I became a huge fan) of a book being made into a television show was Netflix's *13 Reasons Why*.

5)   Music: Even though all of these mediums refer inextricably to tastes and can invoke Pierre Bourdieu's *Distinction*, musical tastes, as I see them, are sporadic. I might have solidified my love for Disney soundtracks through the years, but my love for indie music has increased and my appreciation for Bollywood has declined, just because it has lost its roots and originality. It pulls from all other cultures, especially Pakistani culture, overshadowing it even more.

6)   Movies are inarguably as accessible as television now with the multitude of streaming services available. All of the mediums have genres and ascertain themselves in these genres respectively. What I mean is that a comedy movie would ascertain itself as funny. Books, movies, and television intertwine heavily and feed off each other. For example, books are made into movies.

7)   The internet, ironically, is making us less social. It might not have been conceived that way, so it is allegedly inadvertently doing so, but it is. It is probably conceptually the most social, interpersonal, and communicative medium. It can be viewed as revolutionary and a harbinger of advancements. It is arguable as a flourishing embodiment of a prosperous world; it is ubiquitous. It makes virtually everything—shopping, communicating, arguing, advocating, activism—easier. Does it, however, make speaking easier? Does it

make communicating ultimately more convenient? Even though we are tempted to answer yes, we can say yes *and* no.

It may even be a funny and shocking query to pose if we favor or do not favor the internet.

8) Books are things I use often, because I read profusely. Books are uniquely interesting, because they have evolved and stayed in their respective original format. Publishing books is becoming more convenient and readership around the globe is increasing. The joy of reading is unmatched. This may be a dubious statement to some, but all readers can agree that reading a tactile, physical, original book in its pristine, print perfection has its own inimitable charm.

9) Fashion is probably the most arguably interactive but personal item on the list. We express ourselves through multilayered fashions that can be endlessly interpreted. It is interactive because it is intensely communicative but mostly nonverbal. This is also a convenient and accessible form of diversion. Look down or around before you look in your closet. Fashion provides varying levels of escapism and catharsis, as do books, television, or movies, but it differs in that we physically inhabit it. It inhabits us on physical and mental levels. It feels intrinsic, as we are *in* it.

Fashion is both a form of "human communication" and "self-constitution."[18] The social significance of fashion gives it a substance. To me, this substance is unique to all the other mediums I have listed. This means fashion endows us with meanings and symbols, so we communicate with other beings (not just humans) and demarcate ourselves with weighted meaning.

10) Art, like fashion, is open to interpretation. Is it as dynamic as fashion though? I feel like art can be interpreted dynamically, but it does not change as fashion does. It undergoes a more gradual process of change and evolution,

---

[18] Ford, 7.

but it is a communicative, expressive form of revolt and revolution. All of the other mediums can trace time just like this one and are also forms of revolution, let me note.

Determinism

One of the main functions of this book is to help you recognize blocks to creativity. Creativity, as a concept, is intrinsic, malleable, and ubiquitous. It is infinitely usable and is liberating to use. Determinism is a word I use to describe one of the prominent factors that block creativity. Determinism renders us humans presumptive and predictive. Determinism can be advantageous; it can hurt but also help. It can be a block or a facilitator. One strategy to deal with this determinism and its multiple forms is to prioritize and to keep focus on the process as more fulfilling and imperative than the result. How and why should you do this? You keep your focus on something that has a certain and less elusive presence. This could be something as manifest and assured as the present, which would be the process, and is more fulfilling and satisfying than the future, which is the result.

Examples of the determinisms I talk about are these.

1. Technological determinism inherently also includes weaponry, which is politicized, and I have no intention of discussing politics here. A society is determined by its capacity and/or level of technological advancement. This has an impactful bearing on innovation and imagination. It opens ample doors to ample possibilities. It affects fashion's movement, art's creation, the status of social media, and milieu in general. Technology is a massive indicator for a society's place and path on the nonlinear continuum of life.

2. Cultural determinism: The culture one originates from or resides in plays a tremendous role in either stifling or mediating creativity. The individual has curricula in his or

her culture that ingrain themselves and act to either help or impede creativity. Overall, this determinism is a negative and positive one.

3. Contextual determinism: Time and place are both *transcendent* and *ephemeral*. Interestingly to me, this does not make them uncertain mediums but accentuates their possibilities and potential in existing. This might sound blurry and confusing, so let me elaborate. Time is important and so is place or space. They exist temporarily and have transient existence, but they leave a resolute imprint everywhere. For example, Disney is a place. It evokes times I have spent there and times I've had with it. Disney as a concept and pleasure is resolute and pleasurable in my mind, tirelessly and endlessly.

4. Material determinism: This form of determinism, I envision, intertwined with economic (or socioeconomic) trends and determinism. This form is consistent with the idea of a wasteful society, which I believe we are in the United States. Material determinism is inextricably concerned with escapism and insightful questions about commodification. Of course, not all goods and services are person-to-person or even face-to-face. Not all of them manifest physically or physiologically, making them harder to measure and see. They essentially become invisible, which is highly attributable to society and its future. Material determinism thus determines how a society will use commodities. As Guy Debord says in his work *The Society of the Spectacle*, the society is the spectacle for everyone.[19] We fetishize spectacles, or visual items presented to us. This is also material, and material is often intangible or invisible. Therefore, material determinism deals with two categories of items: those we can see and those we do not necessarily

---

[19] Guy Debord, *The Society of the Spectacle* (Place of Publication: Black and Red, 1967.)

see but can categorize and still sense, even "see" through communicative tendencies from our societies and images.

Conducting therapy in material is directly resonant with a popular saying I use, sometimes in social media captions when I shop: "retail therapy."

5. Ideological determinism is chiefly concerned with institutionalized, sometimes rooted or ingrained, thought, doctrines, or dogmas. What I am thinking of is school, college, or university, or churches, mosques, temples, synagogues, and so on. Religion and knowledge are key factors in this discourse.

6. Linguistic determinism follows grounded parameters. It defines the boundaries of language and culture, especially as it is idiomatic and endemic to inhabitants and constituents of a certain culture. It homogenizes diversified societies like the United States. This is where language takes precedence in a society and controls how the society moves forward. The languages are often part of technology and advancement. This is especially evident and apparent when we assess intergenerational and generational gaps. The reality is akin to the fact that boomers speak a different language than millennials who speak a different language than Gen Z or zoomers (in most respects.)

7. Philosophical determinism is similar to ideological determinism. It is actually the intrinsic facet of ideological determinism. I want to encompass them in different sections so they could be made appropriately and starkly distinguishable. Whatever thought is formulaic in society, or in a certain society, is what encompasses philosophical determinism. This thought is recurringly ascertained by how it works with all of these determinisms.

Philosophies are ingrained in us and circulated in not just physical circles, but in social media. They become habitual as we adopt them. We might even distinguish ourselves by saying we are *skeptics* or *stoics*.

These determinisms, as I may have said before (and may be reiterating), are inextricable to one another; they are intertwined and interdependent.

Sensitivity

I am telling no lies when I say that we are living in a cruel world. Sorry to make the mood all tense now, but people are callous. Of course, there are nice people out there; there are even selfless people and unimaginably selfless people who go out of their way to give you time, attention, or whatever you need. Sometimes, these people provide self-actualization. Do you see how I am lightening the mood but also setting up to talk about how sensitivity is and how I have stopped being sensitive?

An example that mirrors this self-inflicted sensitivity (the kind that is so intrinsic and intrapersonal that it only affects the person in question) is a toothache or consuming cold water or something else the dentist has forbidden. The most imperiling and dangerous fact of sensitivity is desensitization, depersonalization, or derealization. I know the latter two are clinical terms, so I will not use them *clinically* but rather anecdotally. I want to use them in a more everyday context, a social and cultural context. Sensitivity isn't about rendering yourself nonchalant or impenetrable; at least this is not my intention in sensitivity. It is simply about taking care of oneself and others.

Desensitization is scary. It is so imposing as it presents the possibility of a phenomenon that I very much fear, which is normalizing—*even enabling*—heinous and monstrous acts that may event become recurrent. Normalizing the bad is what Trumpkins, as I call them, were best at. They normalized (and Trump chiefly) racism and brought out its most violent and murderous tenets. Sorry if that is offensive to many people, but that is what came to mind immediately.

Depersonalization connotes and denotes multiple things. What I seek to encompass is its tendency to be what it says. It de-personalizes you. You fear people. You fail to connect with people. This can happen to the most extroverted of people; I consider myself an extrovert, and it has happened to me in the past. An unidyllic process, depersonalization is nothing short of menacing and undesirable. When you feel like detachment is key at times, it is usually a last resort type of phenomenon. Detaching yourself from the world or from friends is okay when temporary, when you need to be alone or want me-time, but genuinely diminishing your social networks and growing apart actively is more indicative of something dire and unideal. Going back to depersonalizing yourself, growing detached and/or impersonal is like being a hollow, stagnant form of yourself. This is something you do not want. These terms interplay at the intersection, where they also speak to distancing from people and/or the world. This is tellingly a segue into our next term to assess, which is less commonly used (in my experience) and perhaps more commonplace (exclusively) in clinical circles: *derealization*.

Derealization, most simply, is an altered state. It is, clinically, a disorder, but for our purposes right now, we will consider its status as an altered state. Everything will feel unfamiliar or unreal; make sure to not confuse unreal with surreal. Sometimes surreal and unreal are words attributed to the same thing, because they are elicited by the same things. Surreal is overreal and unreal is not real. The term unreal is used when we cannot fathom something to be part of reality, and surreal is when we think of something as fantastical, ethereal, implausible, or incomprehensible (and maybe unattainable). I think the two words are made indistinguishable and often interchangeable and that this is a subtle and often invisible difference. I wanted to shed light on it moving forward. Derealization deals with unreal ideas, or more specifically, when something becomes unreal to the sufferer. Now that these similar words have been differentiated in order to decipher what derealization is, let us delve into derealization, its facets, and some examples of it. This is not a direct example of the phenomenon (I know calling it a phenomenon gives it a wholly positive connotation but note that this is in no way my intention) but a metaphorical description. Maybe it is an example that manifests itself as a glass wall separating you and others. You (or the sufferer of derealization) are/is living like there is a glass wall separating the sufferer and reality or real word people and contexts.

Spreading the Word

I have to bring in one negative notion: some people are unconvinced of their own creativity or of exercising this art. They are depriving themselves of this amazingly transcendent and revitalizing artform, one that can be implemented and practiced in a multitude of ways. The culture one was brought up in may overlook creativity and an imaginative mindset. This often represses or obstructs one's belief in creativity and blocks his or her own capabilities in reaching his or her potential.

Recognizing the aesthetic realities of the world can help one confront this. A person can recognize his or her own accomplishments; nothing is too minute or minor to create a sense of achievement. Creativity *is* innate, but when one is particularly unconvinced of his or her own creativity, it is dire to instill this belief in the self

Another method in which one can confront the past is to unlearn that he or she is not adequate.

CHAPTER 1

Principles to Live by Revisited

Disclaimer: This chapter will familiarize you with the concepts of how to live a healthy life in therapy. When in therapy, adhering to the principles I present may be helpful. Of course, I do not consider myself an expert. These are considerations that have resonated with my journey as a non-MSW therapy patient living with schizoaffective bipolar disorder.

Principles in Therapy

Everyone has a journey that is unique, characteristic, familiar, and introspective/retrospective to that person. The person will reflect on it in his or her own way, and it is that person's journey to reflect on. While people will have input on that journey, it presents more intimate facets to the person whose journey it is.

There are three principles, and I have categorized them in three phases or terms. They are weighted with their own respective facets and represent different stages. They are acceptance, persistence, and resistance. While I am going to revisit these in depth, acceptance is self-explanatory, but it also involves accountability. It may be the hardest step to take, especially because it is the initial step. Acceptance implies you are responsible for your actions. Even though it is not your fault, the disease of the mind is one that burdens you more than it does others. You have to keep in mind, deeply rooted in your mind, that God Almighty does not burden you with more than you can handle. He has endowed you with a headstrong personality that is capable of enduring what is handed to you. In addition, you will be rewarded for it. You will feel gratified, whether you can foresee it or not. I am attempting to make it foreseeable for you.

Remember the three levels where healing and therapy occurs. This could be any type of phenomenon you feel is therapeutic, transcendent, visceral, surreal, or sensory to you. Alternatively, it can make you have an epiphany or catharsis. These phenomena can happen in sequence by three levels, steps, or capacities: the *micro* level, the *meso* (medium or middle) level, and the *macro* level. These levels, as you can see, go from smallest or largest, but they can intertwine and repeat. For example, on the micro level, there is acceptance. You must accept that you have an addiction or are codependent in some way. You may lose sight of the fact that you need to continually internalize this. When you are living on the meso level, you may see-saw between the meso level and the micro level. Let's get into the three levels now.

i.   **Micro** is the smallest of the three levels. It involves the most rudimentary steps or actions that one undertakes to achieve in therapy. What are some micro things then? When we enact forms of therapy, we must be vigilant and unyielding. This is *our* matter and no one else's. We must be vigilant and watch closely (maybe even intimately) what we are doing and the meaning behind refraining from certain things. Since it is crucial to build upon an understanding of why a therapeutic, healthy lifestyle is better than one full of addiction, abuse, or codependency, we must be assured continually that we matter. This is part of what the micro level encompasses. Therapy will not go away, and it should not. We must work at it for it to fully and holistically help us. They key word here is acceptance. Writing our thoughts down is transformative. Writing can become creative and innovative and prolific. It provides a barrier against our substance abuse and/or codependency. A therapy practice must be built. It will thus become habitual and ritualistic, allowing us to be intimately and inexorably in touch with our creativity.

ii. **Meso** is a less commonly heard term, but it is not hard to understand. Meso is the middle. It is essentially the midpoint between the two other levels. The meso level requires and acquires multiplicities of positive thinking. In the previous level, we received the assurance that a better life is possible without substance abuse or codependency. In this level, while internalizing this message, we build resistance. We make do with the fact that we will not go back to our previous behaviors. They were self-defeating and superfluous. We do not, did not, and will not need them. Now is also the time to explore our creativity and elaborate on it. We may even network it intricately. We must explore forms that we have laid out and decide what is best for us. Whether it is art, poetry, prose, creative nonfiction, playwriting, even roleplaying (yes, because fashion is undeniably a creative and performative medium), it is an outlet. We must singularly and single-handedly decide what works for us, so we must be decisive in this.

iii. **Macro**: We must build upon this all with persistence. This is just the recurrent and endless positivity that we created in the earlier stages. The writing, art, or other form of creativity we are building upon goes further here. Remember, we are human and there is always room for improvement. We must never give up by seeing ourselves as lesser than we are. There is potential in us begging to be unlocked. For example, we can edit our poems, add depth to our characters and/or plot, or revise our artwork through color or composition. Whatever we do, we should do it with (here is another key attribute to have in therapy) enthusiasm.

Putting Yourself First

Before I begin this section, let me remind you that you are your biggest fan, you are your biggest support system, and that you are your protagonist. That statement is a reminder that you are inimitable, influential, and powerful.

You are your priority, so put yourself first. You have to learn that opportunity is available at every point, especially when you look for it. You must unlearn that opportunities do not knock at your door. Of course, some opportunities are more advantageous and providential than others, but opportunities are generally ever-present. As such, you cannot afford to lose yourself. Once you detach from your own self, the process itself snowballs. You direly need to avoid this phenomenon by keeping in touch with your needs and passions and what makes you unique. Losing yourself is irreparable and irrevocable—it is usually inadvertent and unintentional and can feel utterly random and illogical. We look for those to blame for our dissociation and/or disengagement from our existence, reality, and ultimately *ourselves*. The difficult truth is that we are to blame and must hold ourselves accountable.

Toxicity

When we talk about toxicity, it is accurate to say it has become sadly universal and even normal. It is not ideal though. Toxicity involves thought, not just people, and it is not solely perpetuated by extrinsic sources. It can be intrapersonal and internal as well, and we can be utterly toxic to ourselves. Therefore, we make ourselves miserable in this multidirectional, nonlinear process of toxicity. It goes back and forth, no matter who or how many the sources are. Being the toxic source to ourselves is the worst and most imperiling. I can speak firsthand. Toxicity ranges from not accepting ourselves and seeing irreparable flaws to telling ourselves something is too difficult. We may mutter or think phrases like *I'm not good enough* or *I can't*. When toxicity is self-inflicted, it is more aggressive and intense. Why? Because it is a thing of disbelief, and it is surprising when we realize we are the ones hurting ourselves the most. It could even be traumatizing. I invite you to think about it.

Toxicity from others, unfortunately, is inevitable. The fact that toxicity has been made pervasive, ubiquitous, and overall foreseeable is a sad fact; the good news is it is undoable. We can stop being toxic to ourselves and each other, thereby diminishing its overall existence. Coping with toxicity is a tall order because it is prevalent and imposing. It is also quite easy to mask; it masquerades sometimes as a defense mechanism. Toxicity is what some vulnerable people practice. Toxic people like to blame the victim—and act as if they, themselves, are victims—and this is a true mark of a toxic person.

It can be agonizingly traumatic. The distressing memories of a traumatic relationship, whether platonic or romantic, can be evoked at any time. Toxicity is reminiscent of past toxicity; working like a cycle, it builds upon itself the longer it is endured. The sooner one can identify a toxic person or relationship, they quicker he or she can make a strategic exit from it and save himself or herself from stress and others from projected stress. It can even present itself as subtle or innocuous. It can hide in the closets of the most agreeable of people, but they can project it on to you. This always seemed cheesy to me, but then I understood it. When you are surrounded by toxic people, catering to them drains you. They project their toxicities and weaknesses onto you, thus depleting your mental and/or emotional state.

Judgments: To You and From You

Judgments can be complicated. We subconsciously judge and are judged by standards that are ingrained and arbitrarily rooted. We rely on and stick to these judgments, and that is dire and imperiling. We cannot abide by the clichéd and externally influenced judgments we initially make on others. It is not only perilous for us, in a reflexive way (as we might miss out on great people), but it also is damaging and can project onto others. Those others will have new burdens. They must carry an image that no one believes in once the judgment is passed around. This complicates their lives and their livelihoods. It makes living not just harder but even more puzzling. Navigating judgments makes life complicated.

Mindfulness

I want to start this section by reiterating what Qui-Gon Jinn frequently reminds Obi-Wan Kenobi to do in *Star Wars Episode I: The Phantom Menace*: focus on the now.

The future and past can fog your judgment, but in considerably different ways. The future can render you inert or anxious when it is not concrete. The past has happened, and it can bring forth those irrevocable but irrelevant regrets. They are irrelevant because, even though they do matter, they have nothing to contribute to the now, the present.

Transitions

Transitions are perplexing, fleeting, and difficult, but also rewarding and eye-opening. They can start out rough and end well or the other way around. Either way, there is a definite result. Change is inevitable, and so is adapting to those changes. For me, transitions instinctively elicit the term evolution, but here is where I want to be more impartial and neutral, using a term like metamorphosis.

Transitions *are* multidirectional—hence the word *detransition*, like when one is demoted from a leadership position or abdicates the throne. Transitions read in a linear manner but at times can be nonlinear and complex. We expect them to be associated with a duration or timeframe and to move along a traditional timeline. The truth is that transitions elicit so much emotion and insight that they become increasingly complex.

In *Stars Wars Episode I: The Phantom Menace*, when Anakin complains to his mother that he does not want things to change, his mother points to its inevitability. She says, "You can't stop the change, just as much as you can't stop the suns from setting."[20] Even in fictional worlds, there is the notion that change *will* happen.

We are transient and transitory beings; we are endlessly concerned with time and space. We are in flux, even when we least realize it. We are to be innovative and adaptable beings because life calls for these things. Transitions can go forward or backward but are never frozen in time, so to speak. They are not stagnant, in my view, because they are endlessly providing us with new ideals for movement.

Transitions are inherently *transformative*. What we go through in a transition develops us. Now this is not a double-edged sword. It does not take away from us. It equips us with more emotional intelligence. We are able to learn from each transition; whether the transition itself is from a negative source or a positive occurrence or is projected, it will always have at least one ideal takeaway.

Transitioning from a *symbolic* or *metaphorical loss* or "death" is more arduous and intense, and takes longer than transitioning from an actual death or loss. An example of a metaphorical death is a "social death," one in which a person's reputation is tainted. He or she loses identity perhaps. It takes longer to process and is less concrete. It is disembodied, which makes it conceivably elusive; it is hard to grapple with and even grasp.

We *instinctively* resist change, whether is it categorically and wholly good or bad. It is a transition that can be overwhelming. It seems directional. We have to look at it as direction over desperation. We have to act a certain way with change and shift our paradigms and perspectives to fit every change. We also change in three realms: tolerance, taste, and perception.

1.   **Tolerance**: We hopefully and ideally only grow in tolerance. It grows us as we grow with it. We *evolve* and become

---

[20] George Lucas, *Star Wars Episode I: The Phantom Menace*, (1999; Los Angeles, CA: 20th Century Fox, 2005), DVD.

more tolerant. Still, the truth is our tolerance can waver. Tolerance encompasses not only groups but also behaviors. In a different sense, our tolerance for friends or partners who make us feel codependent should ideally decrease. Our tolerances change and either decrease or increase.

2. **Taste**: Our tastes change. I remember when I was younger, I was into music that indicated place. I was only into American music, being a born Californian. My taste expanded; this is a form of change. I grew to love cultural Pakistani popular culture and music. Another example is in my teenage years, I was liked Hollister and Abercrombie. I think this was due to high school compliments on my style when I wore such brands. This slowly faded and I expanded to other brands and styles. I did not necessarily reinvent or redefine my style. It stayed effortful yet looked seamless and effortless, which I realized I could achieve by wearing other brands. Today, I have grown to realize I do not need to wear expensive clothes or top brands to evoke style or dominance in the fashion world.

3. **Perception**: Our view of the vast world is subject to change. It is malleable and susceptible to progress. We flourish through our lens on the world. We do not only have one, and as time goes on, we have more and more. We increasingly alter our perceptions (we change our focus and levels of importance for itemized things) as we learn and unlearn things. We may think a certain food is "icky" and feel like dissociating from it, or we may not like romantic comedies but one day start to admire them.

Heritage: Something of Great Value

Heritage is prematurely and innately possessed. We all have it and it contributes to us and our experiences. This is an entirely different conversation, but some cultures or heritage are maligned and make us feel hesitant to identify with them. I would advise that those who care about you will not judge you based on this but will rather encourage you to identify with your unique position in this diverse world.

In addition, we inhabit a vast, interconnected, and networked world (I emphasize this) where accessibility and availability always come full circle.

What I want to do now is to tackle my favorite passions and pastimes and show how they help me rejuvenate. I was going to include a section on spirituality and how it prematurely cushions falls and pitfalls in our lives, but I fervently believe that religion and spirituality are choices, as I am actively a Muslim.

Conflict, Confrontation, and Compensation

First, the reason I am adding compensation to this section (I am justifying it because it seems random) is 1) to make the title jazzy and alliterative, and 2) to relate it back to conflict.

Conflict is internal and external, and I postulate there are four main types. Usually, these are the types in literature, but they profoundly and appropriately apply to the span and experience of real life. The four types I would like to highlight here are as follows.

1)   The person's or individual's inner struggle(s), or the person versus the self. This is the most weighted struggle, because it is focused on the psyche. A person will confront his or her fate or self-efficacy or may be facing loneliness or emptiness. How we face these ideas ultimately determines out our story.

2)   The individual versus nature (this is the nature aspect of the nature versus nurture debate). This is internal for the most part. The person is struggling or grappling with chaos in the world, with ideals of beauty, or with the abject.

3)   The individual versus society. This points to mores and general ideas society bestows upon us to gauge how we

react to those ideals. This the nurture side of the nature versus nurture debate. Of course, this one points to external struggles.

4)   The last one is the individual versus the individual. In this one, the struggle is overwhelmingly external. The person can be against a foe or even a friend.

A lot of these manifest as binaries. For example, one can struggle with loyalty versus betrayal, honor versus dishonor, hope versus hopelessness, reality versus fantasy, and youthfulness versus aging. Friendship and betrayal occur outside the self while the others are overwhelmingly internal. These are ideals that occur and recur in the mind to a person who is struggling to confront them.

We all have our own ways of compensating ourselves for these struggles. We compensate in ways that are different from coping. Coping is the tactic we employ to relieve ourselves of the struggles. Compensation is how we deal with our new states and maybe even how we reward ourselves. We deserve rewards, after all, since conflict is something we should be proud of confronting and mitigating.

I want to briefly talk about arguments and discussions. We have to be able to acknowledge and distinguish when either is taking place. Discussions are productive and prolific—they create conversations. Arguments render us inert and unable to think forwardly. They incidentally do not create anything novel or favorable; they do not put us in a forward or new direction.

For example, there is the infamous blame game. We play the blame game when we have no one to blame except who we feel is to blame. We, with our human natures, look for someone to blame but our own selves. This does nothing and may even be counterproductive. It has become common to partake in such blame games but, in my opinion, they should be eschewed.

Etiquette and Balance

Balance is one of the most important things in our lives, yet we struggle and strive to maintain it. Balance should mean, as it does to me, one thing: everything in moderation. Overinterpreting a situation is one example of disturbing the balance and causing stress. This could magnify problems by oversimplifying them. Yes, I know that sounds oxymoronic, but it is true. It is reductionist to overmagnify problems by oversimplifying them. A trivial, negligible, or solvable problem can be expanded unnecessarily by a person simply making it more than it is. When we look too closely, we can oversimplify a situation, causing stress.

We possess the tools that equip us with these tools (for therapy.) Problems can be stifling, and they can complicate our journeys in therapy. However, we can make the process positive with what we are given. One term for a tool we can equip ourselves with would be *etiquette.* Another point to make about etiquette is that there is a vernacular for creative people. This vernacular is composed of colloquialisms that are idiomatic only to creatives. Since anyone can find the potential to be creative, the vernacular is universal and can be used in creative pursuits by anyone who adopts it. The vernacular consists of aspirational words and imaginative words. These words are transcendent; they have the potential to open doors and unlock worlds in the expansive creative universe. They are idiosyncratic— they are specific and specialized.

To be an effective creative, it is important that you eschew biases. This way you safeguard yourself from falling victim to confirmation bias and availability bias. Facts, or actually non-facts, will not be able to affect you if you are vigilant about it. To get the most out of therapy, creativity is beneficial. In order to do this, I have looked for inspiration. It lurks everywhere, even in places I least expect it to be. When I am contemplating a new direction or look for my fashion brand, I keep my eyes peeled for inspiration. For this, I know I have to respire and aspire. It is imperative to keep a consistent and coherent tempo for information and inspiration to flow as naturally and programmatically as it can, and to keep an open, flowing mind, which is where aspiration plays an important part.

A final note is on the ethos, pathos, and logos of speech and communication. We also must speak coherently by avoiding disruptive fallacies. One quick concept to learn and apply is balance, meaning being neither too voyeuristic nor reserved or inhibited. This means communicating to a therapist just what you feel. Anyway, let us delve back into the ethos, pathos, and logos. These will, in essence, affect how you speak and how you are responded to. It will catalyze the process of reciprocation, as will proper speech that avoids logical fallacies.

Parallelism

I know this is a literary term, but it resonates with people and transcends its literary use. To me, parallelism means that every action constitutes a reaction of similar or greater magnitude or intensity.

The ways in which we can foster parallelism vary. We can most evidently be down to earth and not let another person feel inferior. We do this by being subtle and hypervigilant in our language in order not to appear patronizing or condescending. We can also physically keep parallelism by our body language and nonverbal communication. We should maintain a tone of peace and stability. By doing this, we keep everyone's anxiety down and do not further induce anxiety or uncertainty in those prone to feel it. We also can extend a hand (yes, literally) by shaking hands or clapping at an accomplishment. This helps keep an atmosphere of support and hopefully of reciprocation.

Bonds

Bonds should be mutual, reciprocal, multidirectional, idiosyncratic, and symbiotic. Often, bonds are based on exchange. I remember being taught that bonds also thrive on proximity, and I would say this constitutes and encompasses both physical proximity and a more philosophical, disembodied, intangible type of proximity.

The fact that they are inherently rooted in exchange and mutuality means that they are nuanced or idiosyncratic. They are characterized by differences and all have their own idiomatic gestures (such as inside jokes, pastimes, secret handshakes, and others).

A great example of this is the phrase, often referred to as an expression of minimalism and used in circles of ecology, that "less is more."

Additionally, bonds are imperatives that put us into groups: in groups and out groups. We belong to in groups that ascertain or align with our identities, and we do not belong to out groups, which differ from our identities.[21] We belong to co-cultures as well, which are more comprehensive, and attribute to us different facets like age, sex, or ethnicity.

Bonds differ in closeness, sadly maybe even in duration. You speak in a different tone and different tensions and elations present themselves in different relationships. In a friendship, you will not make the same remarks or pleasantries you will make in a romantic pursuit. You will still exchange the pleasantries, whether it is with a friend, relative, or lover. With a boss or classmate, these pleasantries will be particular. With rules and codes surrounding you at school, in universities, or in the workplace, you will act differently under the circumstances.

Of course, to bonds, like family bonds, you attribute different ideals. Family is more sanguine and long-standing while friendships will be more candid and sometimes cathartic (since we can talk about things with our friends we cannot talk about with family). This encompasses intimacy, mental, emotional, or physical, in relationships. The duration of a romantic relationship or friendship might waver and be less consolidated than bonds with family.

No relation is impervious to external or internal forces. Whether two people have a dilemma or argument facing them, or a person decides he or she needs time for himself or herself, trouble in bonds is made inevitable by the scheme of things.

---

[21] Adler, Rosenfeld, & Proctor II, 38.

CHAPTER 2
Research and Methods

Therapy is an innately critical process; it is methodological. It seeks not to pathologize but to assesses. When we are creative, we are serving ourselves and hopefully communities at large. In the micro, meso, and macro levels, we assess ourselves and engage in this reflexive process of being innovative people. We endlessly, and maybe even subconsciously, are researching people and society, even when we are being imaginative people. Whether we write or paint or design, we are the architects of tomorrow. It is paradoxical; we engineer the world in a more meaningful way than the literal engineers. We shape the world and construct it with a higher vision that is more rooted and moral. That is not to say that engineers are immoral. That is to say our work is more impactful on a social and cultural scale. Let us delve into a section I think will help us think in a way I do. It will help us think in terms of research and action. It discusses research methods that have to do with therapy and that help us gather information about culture and society. This is information creatives can use to fuel, figuratively or literally, creativity.

As I write in this book, therapy *is* communication, and communication *is* therapy. With that said, interviewing is key in this field. Participant observation will help a therapist assess how a society interacts with participants. Participants become embedded in the culture and society for a duration. Someone who has been in the community knows the culture and internalizes it. He or she is stifled in saying certain things, and the person's identity becomes partly repressed. As therapists are exposed to all of this, they take note and are thus enlightened. This enables them to feel some level of empathy. Of course, empathy is not lived, but it is felt. Unhealthy cultural baggage has made therapy necessary. Sure, I make the point that Pakistan is an overlooked, misconstrued, misjudged, and beautiful country, but our culture, the disembodied representation of the country, is partly toxic. This is monumental and real—very real.

Other than this, interviewing with in-depth and open-ended questions is essential to therapy. Interviewing can even harbor creativity. Therapists and creatives both ask circumspect, thoughtful questions. They ask questions incessantly and ruminate intuitively on the answers, which are never straight, set, defined, or singular. Therapists interview their clients as creatives interview people to assess the state of the world. An innovative person is always an inquisitive person.

 CHAPTER 3

Vignettes

Breaking Tradition

Breaking tradition is very important, since we and our ideals are not extensions of ancestral tradition. We are meant to branch out, and it will undoubtedly be an adventure and experience—an ongoing, lifelong one. We subconsciously have been breaking tradition. We do not realize it because we do not mean any harm. Breaking tradition is uncertain and can be challenged, but what is resolute is that fact that it forgoes being rigid or myopic or conventional. Breaking tradition does not mean breaking away from tradition. I still happen to be enormously invested in the idea of heritage, as mine remains intimately woven into my life.

Breaking tradition is done by means that are easy but also difficult. A person may feel apprehensive about being looked down upon or chastised. For example, I wore distressed jeans to the mosque. People admired me for my bravery, considering the sensitivity of the situation and how courageously I challenged it. I have been wearing this studded denim jacket from Zara that I love at family gatherings, and my mom tells me I cannot be edgy in front of relatives. However, I feel so liberated and comfortable in my details.

Breaking tradition is liberating; that is not debatable, at least not to me. It is more than that though; it expands our horizons and opens doors we never imagined existing. It unlocks worlds and worldviews. It also breaks tedium and monotony, exposing us to new settings in our heads and in our bodies.

Scenarios

Do you ever feel like you arbitrarily make scenarios in your head that may never happen? I have realized they could. Thus, they are not arbitrary or unattainable, and I learned that through experience. In fact, I happen to believe that having fantastical scenarios in our heads is therapeutic in that they motivate us and help us flourish. They makes us feel that we are prospering or progressing.

For example, when I was young, I would pray and dream of having at least one book published. Hopefully this one is published. However, the fact that I have published poetry books and self-publishing is now available to make me more prominent in the literary arena prove that nothing is impossible. It proves to me I can do what I set my mind to.

This is not so much a scenario as a mainstay and/or a disclaimer for life in general. You are not trite. You are not banal, no matter what. You are the main attraction. After all, as William Shakespeare very famously said, "All the world's a stage." You are noteworthy and buzzworthy.

You may wonder how everyone can be the main attraction, but assuredly you are. Everyone has the capacity and chance to be a main character as his or her story and journey unravels. You are unique and distinct and embark on countless adventures. As you are a protagonist—a main character—your story involves events and climaxes and multiple resolutions.

As such, your story consists of antagonists. These are roadblocks that can be manifested as people or beings or even just simple hurdles. They can be dismissive naysayers; they can be animate or inanimate. The fact is that these are temporary and are made and presented to us to be conquered. We can only gain when we conquer them.

Stream of Consciousness

As humans, we tend to think in an erratic, impatient way. We can often draw out a stream of consciousness from our minds. Of course, this sporadic pattern is not abnormal; it is human nature. We string together the thoughts we are consciously thinking, but I would say our subconscious thoughts and longings are equally important.

It is important for us to pay attention to how impulsively we act on a thought. Some of us have more obsessive or addictive personalities and capacities than our peers. As such, if we perceive, for example, that fashion defines us—"I shop therefore I am"—we internalize it. We act on those impulses and spend on clothes in excess, sometimes arbitrarily. This is a weakness I have. My other one is Disney and my novelty collections. Basically, when I log onto my Shop Disney app, I find something that compels me to buy. I favorite the item or items and add them to my favorites. Because I have no control over my Disney obsession, the items end up in my cart and I buy them eventually. I fetishize and romanticize my life with those items, and I do not think they will be inadequate for me or defective. Soon, I am so wanton and impetuous about an item that I cannot live without it, even though I have not even had a moment with it. This is why our thoughts often *betray* us in a way; I know that is a cliché. We have to be vigilant about our desires and not be tempted. We have to learn that we can live without that item and we have been thriving without it.

Existence, Questions, Musings, and The Universe

Our existence is debatable. Debating and questioning our own existence produces peculiar feelings. One thing is for certain: our existence is not arbitrary or meaningless. We all have a purpose and a calling. Try not to wonder about it; let it be a given that you are worthy and capable and purposeful.

Some questions I have are these. *How finite or infinite is the world or our world (our perceived and personal world or universe)? What are its limits and/or extents? Why are we not content with our earth?* We seem to be insatiably longing for, seeking, or locating more territory than just Earth. We are always exploring space and arguing for the colonization of other planets, namely Mars.

I also wonder what it means to be someone's "universe." I guess that is a special and fraught weight to give someone. It sounds ridiculous and preposterous to throw this out there, but when one is loved and admired in that way, it makes that person susceptible to being reduced to a mere ideal.

CHAPTER 4

Minutiae and Miscellany

Me Time

Sociologists have coined the term "me time," although we throw it around casually but indispensably. Me time (time for oneself) is certainly something we all need; it is chiefly reflective. It is not only time to reflect, but it is therapeutic. We move as transitory beings through present and past tense, so me time is part of mindfulness.

Intelligence, Attachment, and EQ

How does intelligence really work? How do we communicate our own intelligence intelligibly or articulately rather than just the concept of intelligence? How does our language of intelligence coordinate and/or correlate to the type of intelligence being employed? These questions have provoked me for a long time, so let's delve into them. Let us also supplement this exploration into intelligence, namely the languages and forms of intelligence, with types of attachment and how it all interrelates and intertwines. We can also see how we intertwine them. In doing so, we will invoke and call upon the ideas and work of sociologist George Herbert Mead.

All types of intelligence are distinguishable from each other but are certainly interlaced, just like the personality styles. For instance, my Myers-Briggs personality is ENFP (Extraverted, Intuitive, Feeling, and Perceiving), so I consider myself an extrovert. At times, I feel timid or shy, so I have attributes related to being an introvert as well. Someone with dispositions toward extroversion and an introversion can be classified as an ambivert. Though ambiverts are more hidden, they are just as real and valuable.

Linguistic-verbal intelligence can most closely intertwine with bodily-kinesthetic intelligence. When using them together, we can unlock a more encompassed, visceral, multisensory state. Together, these intelligences can speak to the embedded, embodied, and intangible facets of the human experience and how our awareness of the entire experience and its parts interact.

Attachment and styles of attachment may be causes of a dominant style of intelligence in a person. Attachment and intelligence are both concepts that have several forms that interweave and interrelate. There are three types of attachment: secure attachment, avoidant attachment, and anxious attachment. People who are anxiously or avoidantly attached have had a childhood of possible trauma, neglect, and/or abuse, and they find it challenging to have intimacy.

Securely attached people approach intelligence in a less timid, more wary, and collected manner.

As I emphasize in this section, attachment is better than a lonely, empty, or debilitating feeling. Something is better than nothing, and in most cases, even with relationships this is conceivable and ideal. The main time when it is not ideal is when the relationship (whether platonic, romantic, or something else) is toxic and should not exist. I like to reference *Star Wars* a lot, and again here it is. Jedis have to forgo attachment. I cannot cite a specific movie in the franchise for this because it recurs. The reiteration comes from a phrase attributed to Buddha: "attachment is the root of suffering." Sometimes, it is healthy not to cling to an attachment or bond. Some bonds in life are better eschewed. Make no mistake: they are not better to forget. Why is that? We must learn from our pasts and have no regrets. The question is "Who are you?" to partly quote Rafiki in *The Lion King*. To further reference his wisdom, we all have a past, and we can either leave it behind completely or as Rafiki states, "learn from it."[22]

Now I will talk about EQ, because it is an enormously important measure of one's capacities. We are barraged with the concept of

---

[22] Roger Allers and Rob Minkoff, *The Lion King* (1994; Burbank, CA: Buena Vista Pictures, 2003), DVD.

IQ, or intelligence quotient, throughout life, to measure how smart or intelligent we are. I remember taking the IQ test when I was in elementary school. I also remember taking IQ tests online. I never heard of EQ tests to measure someone's emotional intelligence; that is what EQ is. There is no doubt in my mind that it is as important as the idea of IQ. Just as an IQ would measure how you deal with situations in life, so does EQ. EQ is as important because it is as *impactful* and *meaningful* in life. EQ is not a quantifiable number like IQ; neither are arbitrary measures, but they are both nuanced. EQ is such because it changes sporadically and applies to differing contexts and conditions. These idiosyncrasies make EQ characteristically hard to measure.

Politics of Love

We learn to love by the act of love itself in all of its simplicity. Our goal is never to hate, but we might veer towards hate when we just want to get someone out of our heads. We might still love them or the time we had with them. This is the healthiest way to achieve closure in a scenario that is oriented towards love. We engage in lexicons of love and languages that codify it. We might have picked up habits from past lovers, and those are the so-called politics we should focus on.

When we feel like we have loved someone so intensely and that person may have become an intractable, infallible part of our lives, we just have to remember that he or she is moving on and has every right to live. We do too, so we move on as well. The other person's world will not stop and neither should ours.

On Platitudes

When I consider how many times a day and in how many different settings platitudes are used, it is a bit evasive. The fact is that they can be reductive. They are unnecessarily reassuring because they are *too* optimistic and too deceptive. There is obviously nothing wrong with being ambitious or optimistic, but pointing out that too much of this good thing is a bad thing does not mean I am being pessimistic. Platitudes should be used in moderation because they can delude our thinking. Platitudes should be sought with care and not readily canonized. They are not ubiquitous and do not encompass the common population. They can paint a false mosaic that we should never doom ourselves to follow.

Mnemonic Devices

Mnemonic devices are indispensable in so many respects. They are often used in the context of studying; I remember many of them from school. Two of the most evident examples are PEMDAS, for order of operations, and KFCFGS, for the animal kingdom. PEMDAS stands for Please Excuse My Dear Aunty Sally for Parentheses, Exponents, Multiplication, Division, Addition, and Subtraction. KFCFGS is King Phillip Came Over for Green Soup for Kingdom, Phylum, Class, Family, Genus, Species. They make the incomprehensible more accessible in simplistic terms and help us follow them, not just remember them. In a broader sense, mnemonic devices help us navigate complex ideas and relate to them and vice versa.

To cite an example of my own for therapy and social circles, I want to bring in three words that should constitute the flow of talk and of communication. I am proposing and promoting the acronym ARC for Articulate, Resonate, and Cohere. This helps you delve into what another person is feeling, whether you are a therapist dealing with a client or a friend dealing with another friend.

23

Articulate—The word *articulate* means that people permit themselves to express themselves and their feelings and to talk freely and candidly.

Resonate—Make every statement by the other person or party relate to you; feel it deep within you. Be relatable and feel the other person's every insight and emotion.

Cohere—Make sure not to let anything impede, intrude on, or disrupt the flow of communication. Words should transition from one to the other and connect with one another.

CHAPTER 5

From Beginnings: Being Pakistani

I am proud to be a Pakistani-American Muslim. I take vocal pride in my heritage. I feel authentic connections to this culture. I am fluent in Urdu, despite being born in Riverside, California. I love Pakistani music, dress, and food. Being Pakistani does not guarantee being Muslim, but being both means so much to me and has taught me I have much to contribute to a polarized world on all levels. Being authentically Pakistani allows me to resonate with my heritage and hopefully encourages other Pakistanis to adopt the same keen willingness to identify with being Pakistani.

Aside from all the positives I have been highlighting, it is imperative that I provide information and my insights on the negative side, namely the cultural and generational baggage. Sometimes the culture can be overwhelmingly toxic, stifling, and overbearing. While the culture is vibrant and colorful, with a revival in the film industry and amazing fashion, there is a stark, dire, and dim reality that Pakistan's new generations of diaspora confront. Policing happens and can be extreme. That is taken lightly by older generations, and newer generations grapple with it on a daily and consistent basis. This patronizing can be detrimental and is undoubtedly myopic and limiting to the policed (the youth). It can have effects that are otherwise invisible because they are manifest in the mental health of a person and thus irrevocable. This makes one feel watched; it necessitates hypervigilance.

Of course, heritage and belonging are complicated by a polarized world. As resonant to us and endemic to us as they are, as reminiscent of identity and positionality as they are, they are ambivalent, especially heritage. Heritage, namely, is ambivalent because it is rooted in the past but indicates movement of values in the present. Heritage of any kind comes with countless precursors and preconceptions. Notional and preconceived, they are ill-informed and make us go backwards. Heritage is a beautiful thing that we all ascribe to but unfortunately, inadvertently, and usually innocuously denounce. Heritage is something we want to be proud of, but we find it increasingly hard to do so. The world is a fragmented, hollowed carcass and shell of what it ideally has been but never was. Delving into one's own heritage is enlightening, telling, and didactic, but it is also eye-opening and all-encompassing as an experience and adventure. Heritage unravels naturally for everyone. Heritage, no matter what type, is a denotative word in the end. After all, it is a powerful entity and should be looked at in all its facets, not as a monolith or as something much worse: baggage.

Pakistani people carry trauma and baggage but suffer in silence. They do not normalize but rather stigmatize the idea of *sharing*. Sharing is literally caring. Sharing causes catharsis in people and people might gain catharsis from hearing others *share*.

I am sure it has been said before, *because* it is so important. We need a curriculum to teach people how to deal with their pasts—not just their pasts, but the historical, inherited past that is so weighted. However, the past also provides people with good things. For example, I really love spicy food and my heritage is all about spicy food. My heritage has given me the disposition for thinking forwardly and redefining conventional ideals because it was so rooted in toxic conventions. Heritage also gives us trauma—inherited trauma that we have learned to cultivate because we have lived with it. We need a systemic, programmatic way, like a curriculum, to combat trauma. We need to be able to look at the positive capacities and facets of our heritage so we do not reject them. I have people who are dismissive of their own heritage, reluctant to even recognize it, when it is something they are missing. We need to devise a way, not specifically educational or academic, for people to cope with and ultimately confront cultural, mental, and multigenerational trauma.

A dilemma facing first-generation youth in a country like the United States is an us versus them mentality, which can be paraphrased as "you are either with us or against us." This is recurrent, constant, and ambivalent, and I can attest to it. It can be arbitrarily politicized, and it can spread to ideas of status, ownership of land and property, and hierarchies. It causes separation. We can combat it by not internalizing it or allowing it to fester and perpetuate. Additionally, the us versus them dilemma cuts deep. It piques, provokes, and pokes constantly at us, begging us to find a resolute answer to the never-ending and complex question of who is a foreigner and who is a native. I have studied colonialism in a few cultural and ethnic studies classes, so I have to acknowledge the terms *settlers* and *colonists*. It is confusing when you begin to question where you fall in these categories. I feel America is my land; I was born here in California and lived here my entire life. I sometimes am made (by the media, by peers' comments) to feel like a foreigner, and it is alienating. An American, southern Californian by birth, I am still othered because I have brown eyes and jet black hair. I have tan skin and Pakistani features, and no matter how confidently and boldly I wear them, I inadvertently invite and elicit comments that will make me feel alien. I am Pakistani-American, and I can fit both molds, being a total Pakistani at times and at other times being a blend of both. I am not a foreigner; my parents are, and I am not (keep in mind) an exact extension of them or their mannerisms.

I love many facets of my heritage and many of my birth country and culture. I sometimes feel conflicted, like I am picking and choosing, and that it is wrong. The truth is that both sides of this co-cultural, constructed identity are beautiful. They contribute to my self-concept. My way to cope with a dual identity is to recognize that my self-concept, which I control, is the presiding factor in the ongoing conversation. It has given me the ability to cope with the negatives my dual identity might throw at me.

Does being in a certain cultural/ethnic group affect the way your story is told and heard? The answer is *yes*. This may sound like I am foreshadowing negative outcomes, but there are positives to it. Your heritage has valuable and unique facets. This sounds clichéd, but it is true. Your heritage equips you with techniques, like paradoxes and existential questions, to help you narrate your existence. One paradox might be a cultural expectation to pursue intellectual excellence but not personal growth. These experiences invite us to ask how not to feel suffocated or how to feel liberated. The negative forces that affect how stories are told are intrusive and less intrusive. They can be internal or external. People may perceive our stories as "colored" (that is, told by people of color) and to be maligned and marginalized. Nonetheless, we must remember that our stories are not to be pushed away. They are inextricable to the world, significant, precious, and useful, and we must tell them with active conviction. We must not feel disconsolate, because our stories will suffer. It is imperative that our stories be told, and we must be vigilant as they are not impervious to outside judgment or inside self-rejection. Loving ourselves is another way to love our stories. They are *our* journeys, respectively and entirely ours.

Our stories all carry a specialized, significant weight. This weight, however, is not all negative. Yes, I know that the word *weight* implies that there is baggage that holds us down. However, I do not believe where we come from and our lives' events hold us down more than they pick us up. They can function as avenues for benefitting the world through our own retrospective pasts, intuitive presents, and projected futures. They can be avenues for collective and reciprocal growth and change.

One last note is that our stories assimilate into the mainstream or into popular culture, gaining traction and hope. However, they take a little longer to assimilate because they have an allure of being foreign, even if they originate here in the United States. They need to not be demonized or reduced so they can be enlightening and authenticated.

CHAPTER 6

Being a Disdork: My Disney Obsession

Disney is a monumental and *healing* part of my whole identity. It is a part, but a significant part. Disney makes me feel whole. While some critics have said Disney is reductive, I would say it is necessary. It makes the stories that it adapts its own.[23]It has power to heal and provide therapy. More than anything, I know Disney is the passion in my life that gives me the most pleasure; in fact, even writing about it does. It makes me part of the conversation.

Whether it is the animation or parks, it is totally its own. There is always something "missing" if you go elsewhere.[24] Walt Disney was a masterful storyteller with a revered legacy. People argue and are upset that his stories portray the world in a reductionist, overly "happy" light with songs and happy endings, but isn't that what we need? We need to stop thinking of the world as a dreary, morbid place that is completely flawed and uninhabitable. Stories that were originally grotesquely gloomy and starkly glum became Disney stories—approachable, accessible, and most importantly, joyful and happy.

For example, *The Fox and The Hound* was based on Daniel P. Mannix's story of the same name.[25] In the original, Tod the fox has his vixen killed. He procreates again and has the entire family killed. The widow Tweed is changed from a vile hunter who kills his family into a loving and protective caretaker.[26]

Disney is a perfect embodiment of the cliché that life imitates art. Disney resonates with viewers because it is a medium in itself. It

---

[23] David Koenig, *Mouse Under Glass: Secrets of Disney Animation and Theme Parks* (Irvine, CA: Bonaventure Press, 2015), 14.
[24] Koenig, 14.
[25] Koenig, 166.
[26] Koenig, 167.

imitates life with its art by embodying morals, themes, and motifs in its productions and spaces.

How do I feel when I visit a Disney theme park? I like to be the one with more experience, even though I love going with people who are admittedly more expert at Disney than I am. I like being the map; it makes me feel empowered. I know all of the perks and how to get around. I have heard countless times, "We don't need a map. Umar is the map!" It makes me feel so precious.

CHAPTER 7

Fervid about Fashion:
Catharsis through Couture

Fashion is associative and transformative. It is chiefly three things. It is associative because it embodies networks and connections. It is transformative because it can have multiple effects on the user, especially mental and physical. Fashion can equip the wearer with a vehicle for expression of identity or personal statements. It is performative because it enlivens the wearer and his or her surroundings. When we don fashion, we recontextualize and rejuvenate ideas and concepts. It has endless potential to engrain and manifest itself in any society or group; it fills our voids of desire and is approachable and visible.

Fashion is not only my therapy and my passion, but it has a power to bring out authenticity in people and even (in my case) bridge gaps to my aforesaid heritage. My heritage is Pakistani. Pakistani designer Hasan Sheheryar Yasin, owner of the brand HSY, makes me feel an intrinsic link to my heritage. He gave a 2021 TED Talk in which he claimed that innovation is related to authenticity and is internal. He said that we become inauthentic very quickly and people resonate through what is genuine and authentic. He said his brand is truly Pakistani and that it represents Pakistani woman, not the canonized Parisian fashion icon.[27]

Although fashion has been favorable to me, and I speak of it positively, I also have to say that behind the glitz, history, glamor, and glory is a critical side. When we look at this side however judgmentally or methodologically, teasing out the intricate,

[27] Hasan Sheheryar Yasin, "Being Innovative by Being Authentic," filmed May 2021 at TEDxSaddarRoad, Rawalpindi, Pakistan, video, 17:57, https://www.youtube.com/watch?v=LlNxaXsWupE.

circumspect pathologies that can be overlooked but not ignored or negotiated, we feel rewarded and more wary. Fashion has a nasty side, often substantiated, supplemented, and supported by its complicated, multifaceted history.

I am going to be harsh and list reasons why I think fashion can be harmful. They help explain why fashion is subconsciously damaging.

1.   Cultural appropriation is the most evident and harmful (in my opinion) of the effects. Fashion can fight racism and cultural appropriation, but as a double-edge sword, can also encourage it. Examples include Justin Bieber sporting cornrows, Marc Jacobs' white models sporting vibrantly colored dreadlocks,[28] and Katy Perry's "Dark Horse" music video. It is a toxic and pervasive practice. Even though I absolutely adore the spooky (not scary) side of Halloween, Heidi Klum's costumes on Halloween are offensive and foster a culture and atmosphere of toxicity.

2.   Fashion can be exclusionary. Historically, the elites distinguished themselves by fashion. Nowadays, subcultures disrupting social order and challenging canons of discourse[29] are the issue. Cliques are created, not just in high school but in society, and there is an in group and an out group. As Richard Thompson Ford claims, "fashion's status symbols still mark the traditional allegiances of class, kinship, faith, and nation. But they are also signs of individual personality and symbols of affinity for cliques, gangs, subcultures, and countercultures."[30] It is alienating at the least to be part of the outgroup. Social desirability thus plays a role. This complicates sartorial therapy and creativity by virtually

---

[28] Cherise Smith, "Cultural Appropriation is Everywhere. But Is it Always Wrong?" *Time*, September 21, 2016, https://time.com/4501037/cultural-appropriation-marc-jacobs-dreadlocks/.

[29] Dick Hebdige. "The Unnatural Break," in *Media and Cultural Studies*, ed. Meenakshi Gigi Durham and Douglas M. Kellner (New York, NY: Wiley. 2001), 144.

[30] Ford, 353.

coercing people to belong to a sartorial group, rather than have their own respective identities and styles (which is necessary and therapeutic).

Sure, my criticism of those who think of fashion as "superficial" or "trivial" seems impermeable. These people calling the fashion industry ignorant for different reasons are being myopic and hypocritical. Fashion can be informative, insightful, and didactic.

Fashion is an extension of language. When we want to communicate something about ourselves or our conditions (or, for that matter, the condition of the world), we can use fashion. We can use it to challenge laws of society, like dress codes or hierarchies. We can use it to be walking billboards directly or even indirectly. Of course, we can see the power in fashion. It may be a long journey for some people to see, but it is there. Fashion has power and is utterly transformative. In this way, it is beneficial. Ford also says,

> Our clothing can transform us from object into citizen; it can remake our interactions from bestial struggle for survival into an Enlightened competition for excellence; it can elevate our sexuality from an animalistic urge into an expression of poetic connection; it can turn a social obligation into a glamorous adventure; it can make the solitary daily grind into a stylish personal biography.[31]

To me, the most therapeutic part about fashion is that it is a vehicle for diversity. To me, diversity is not just a prerogative; it is not just an initiative; it is not only a concept that is necessary but dire. Even if modeling and the industry doesn't always stand by diversity, conceptually fashion is diverse. Ford says,

> The history of dress codes tells the story of medieval cross-dressers, Elizabethan upstarts, Renaissance

---

[31] Ford, 358.

courtiers, and colonial American slaves dressing
above their condition; of Victorian dandies, industrial
era social climbers, seriously sexy flappers, and
disaffected zoot suiters; of earnest activists in their
Sunday best, chic radicals, and radical feminists; of
blonde African American bombshells, and natural
blondes in dreadlocks; of hipster *hijabis*, preppy street
gangs, and high-tech fashionistas.

He ends by saying those who pioneered such fashions and
conditions have given us something valuable even when they were
not understood in their respective time.[32]
Fashion still has a reach like no other medium does. In therapy,
isn't that connection and engagement with people what we crave
and need? It is mobile, citing the walking billboard metaphor again.
An example of this is someone wearing a t-shirt that supports a
movement; more people are susceptible to seeing it. This is active and
proactive advertising. The person can be embroiled in the movement
itself, and can engage with it and with the thought process behind it.
For example, a person can ask the individual why he or she supports
the movement or cause or what it means to him or her. The individual
can elaborate on it, thus empowering and esteeming himself or
herself.
Another appreciable trait of fashion is its potential to be three
things: a conversation or discourse itself, a conversation piece, and
a conversation starter. It is understandable that it can be difficult to
discern between these, but I will make them distinguishable in the
succeeding lines of this book. Before I do, I would like to add that
fashion is exciting—there's never a dull moment. Essentially, fashion
is always on the move and is far-reaching with its seemingly endless
mobility and visibility.

---

[32] Ford, 369.

Now let us dive into the three traits I just mentioned.

1. Fashion as a conversation or discourse: Fashion is increasingly academic. It has made its place in the philosophical spectrum. It has gained traction as an interdisciplinary and intertexual field of study. It is not only mobile, but it mobilizes the person studying it. It lets the person delve into concepts and ideas of aesthetics and insightful thought.

2. Fashion as a conversation piece: This is a more visual and technical aspect of fashion. Material items can be conversation pieces. They can facilitate and mediate ideas between garments, or in this case, as I have termed them, picces.

3. Fashion as a conversation starter: Fashion starts critical conversations that are overlooked as started by fashion. Whether it is a student or academic examining it or a bystander or a pedestrian wearing or witnessing it, fashion is that conversation starter to begin, arbitrate, and negotiate ideas and discourse. Fashion may have aspects to it that make it seem trivial, but I question if it really should be looked at as such at all.

I claim that fashion is a figurative device. It has ample symbologies and is synecdochic of myriad concepts and items. Fashion is symbolic of society and time, the zeitgeist, social hour, and communication climate. It is synecdochic of things and can function as other figurative devices, such as metonymies, verisimilitudes, and hyperboles. "Suits" refer to businesspeople. This is metonymy.

Another more specific and specialized way in which fashion is beneficial is in media. I know I characterized media as a monstrous entity that can impede creative and therapeutic endeavors. However, in some aspects fashion can work in tandem with media to create and promote creativity. Remember, I did say it is a double-edge sword: it contains good and bad traits. In social media or the blogosphere, fashion becomes more ubiquitous and pervasive. Fashion is first a game, or a "serious game" as coined by Clifford Geertz in his essay "Deep Play: Notes on Balinese Cockfight."[33] It is a game because it teaches in a fun way. In the blogosphere and social media, we have street style and hashtags like OOTD or OOTN. We create a fashionable community in this manner. We are self-reflexive in blogging and documenting our styles. Luvaas references the term auto-ethnography, coined by Karl Heider in 1975, to say we delve into ourselves with this process. [34] Fashion, thus, does not only please the world at large is personally meaningful and pleasurable. It also teaches us about ourselves; it makes us intuitive about ourselves and so many other concepts.

Fashion can help confront pressing and trending issues that really matter.

Fashion can also further ideas. As mentioned before, "less is more" is a parallel statement. In time, we see the two relate. More and less are complete opposites, yet less is attributable to "more" because it perpetuates and indicates abundance. Fashion is a prime example because the fewer garments one has in his or her closet, the more room for creativity he or she has. Making a few garments work shows how a person can make his or her limited choices work and weave them into an ensemble or an outfit that is impeccable or bespoke.

Fashion allows you to be impeccably and incredibly alluring. It allows you to carry eccentric concepts inside yourself while perpetuating, circulating, and creating conversations. It begs insightful questions that provoke and evoke more thought and discourse. It amply answers its own questions.

Advantages of fashion are many and are often overlooked; they can be described as hiding in plain sight. As Otto von Busch says in his book *The Psychopolitics of Fashion: Conflict and Courage Under the Current State of Fashion*, fashion can help us engage with what he calls social cognition. He points to the way fashion can help us navigate

---

[33] Geertz, Clifford. "Deep play: Notes on the Balinese cockfight." *Daedalus* 101, no. 1 (1972): 1-37.

[34] Brent Luvaas, *Street Style: An Ethongraphy of Fashion Blogging* (London: Bloomsbury Academic, 2016), 11.

this intricate, fragmented, complex world. It can help us make sense of our surroundings in the social contexts that we are presented.[35]

Additionally, my writing has prompted me to ask what makes good or ideal fashion. My short answer is that fashion should be three things: investigative, narrative, and philosophical. It has to consider a providential future and tell a story. It has to answer questions. It meticulously considers smaller intricacies, subtleties, and minutiae, but it also has to focus on bigger-picture elements. It has to encompass bigger implications and the zeitgeist (social hour or spirit of the times) that it exists within. Remember that it does not exist in a vacuum or in isolation. Good fashion involves and immerses its consumers, patrons, or aficionados.

It is also three other things. It is resonant because it helps people feel a resounding and grounded connection to it. It is relevant because it speaks about time and puts the consumer/aficionado into the conversation of fashion. It is corporeal. Fashion should compose a body of and for beings and make us all feel part of the body. It should also be physically present in the idea that people advertise it and are walking billboards. In essence, fashion should always read as worldly, collectivistic, and ubiquitous.

Fashion is certainly a double-edged sword, with negative and positive facets and implications for us. We should look to adopt the positive facets as our habits. In this way, fashion becomes increasingly ritualistic. We routinely develop the habits that serve us and make for a prescient, sustainable future. Fashion can help us learn favorable habits and unlearn unfavorable habits. We can practice, preach, or even perpetuate these habits. We can thus inspire others to follow our practices, like spurning excess, spending wisely, or being eco-friendly or promoting diversity. We, in turn, can placate the fashion world and make its negative points recede.

Fashion, lastly, is a therapeutic realm as it naturally lets us inhabit it. It reiterates that mimicry is the best form of flattery—I know, an

---

[35] Otto von Busch, *The Psychopolitics of Fashion: Conflict and Courage Under the Current State of Fashion* (London: Bloomsbury Visual Arts, 2020), 81.

overdone cliché. It's true though, and fashion redefines such clichés. We should think of others more as inspired or influenced by us in positive, monumental ways, and we will feel better. I know I have influenced people to pay attention to their wardrobe choices; they want to feel better, because they see my confidence has soared while my style has evolved.

CHAPTER 8

About Aesthetics: Art

It is daunting to write about art. It is always evolving but also it is intertwined with multiple other mediums. I appreciate art. It is not unstable, but it reaffirms shared ideas and identities. It is also questionable in the way that we all interpret it differently. We all take something uniquely different from art pieces. Writing about art might be challenging, but it is also distinctively rewarding and cathartic; this goes for reading about art as well. As with fashion, art has aesthetic and philosophical components. It encourages rumination while simultaneously giving the onlooker a spectacle. The spectacle is societal in that it can make historical or cultural commentary, and it is a vehicle for being not just expressive but wholesome and vocal. It is an engagement and interaction between artist and the onlooker.

It is one of the creative mediums, but it is highly lucrative and institutionalized. It is what might instinctively come to mind when we hear or think of the terms in creativity, because it is always present. I am not as invested in art itself as I am in the arts. Art is distinguishable by its static properties, but it does not stagnate. Interestingly, art is on the move. It is a more gradual and experiential movement than that of fashion, but art certainly travels, alters, and moves.

Art is a timeless medium, similar to other mediums, and is also a time capsule. It has gained popularity in the past, and this has been due to the monetary investment in it. It is worthy, significant, and worldly. Art weaves together subcultures.[36] It resonates with people and they believe in its power. It has ageless qualities that give it ample power and abundant potential.

---

[36] Sarah Thornton, *Seven Days in the Art World* (New York: W.W. Norton and Company, 2009), xi.

Let me assert that art can be intrapersonal (speaking to the artist) or interpersonal (fostering a conversation or dialogue between artist and onlooker). Art can be meaningful to the artist in unique ways inscrutable to the onlooker. These are less common than interpersonal iterations that art piece would have and convey. It is passive, still, and inert. Fashion is an art, but art itself is not mobile like fashion and thus does not have the same type of reach. Given this, art is still exceptionally potent, salient, and visceral. It has been around since the Lascaux cave paintings and has served numerous purposes. It is potent because it can easily make immensely strong statements. It is inherently existential but can avoid this. It can still make existential statements and also cultural, political, and social statements. It can work toward betterment and improvement of humanity and human interactions.

Art, in its most kinetic and physical renditions (something I call experimental art) is directly attributable to Susan Sontag. She deals with space, as does her art. Art that deals with space may deal with time as well—the social clock or mood or zeitgeist. Art makes statements, and art can be starkly unnamable and uncategorizable. Fashion, compared to art, has an alluring, compelling mystique that one can therapeutically marvel at, and both art and fashion inhabit spaces and time.

I don't know why I am tempted to say this, but art is more readily traceable than fashion. The reason is that academia regards art and does not regard fashion; fashion is novel to academia as it has been seen as trivial. Art, when we consider its history, traces back to cave paintings in Lascaux, France, and the Venus of Willendorf. According to Susan Sontag, in her 1966 essay "Against Interpretation," the reminder given is that art started with mimesis and mimetic theory.[37]

I want to end the section by beginning (or continuing) the conversation that some items in the world have such a compelling aesthetic quality that they cause us to rejoice or experience a certain delirium. We may experience euphoria or epiphany, but certainly this carries with it an ambivalence.

---

[37] Susan Sontag, *Against Interpretation and Other Essays* (New York: Dell, 1966), 3.

CHAPTER 9

Ears Embody Me: Music

The clichéd and trite saying has it that laughter is the best medicine. Although that is certainly not a farfetched or overdone platitude, I believe firmly that it is safe to say music is too. Why else would we have the term eargasmic? I want to elucidate my stance on and appreciation for music here because it is primarily what seeped deeper into me in my depression, pulling me out of it.

Music certainly is universal; it is a language just like other arts are. It brings up the question of taste. It can be eclectic or by-the-book. One can be very loyal to one genre of music and explore that, or be experimental and widespread in his or her taste. My taste is for alternative or indie music. I started out loving rock music but I branched out into more subgenres in the indie genre. I consider it all rock to make it more easily categorizable, but this category encompasses art indie pop, indie rock, art pop, art rock, and others.

EPILOGUE

My sound advice (which might sound like common sense) is to not be dismissive (even when it could be inadvertent or unintentional) of your feelings. It can be so momentous for someone to open up and let you in. It is a privilege for you and a step (to whatever extent and size) for that person when he or she shares. Make sure the other person feels validated and heard. Being flippant or aloof can also be taken as mocking. When a person feels like he or she is being mocked, the person will change to a more defensive tone. This can create commotion and disorder in the conversation.

It is a positive note that our stories do not need hooks. They definitely have them, but all we need are listeners. We need active, attentive listeners. We do not need perfect listeners but ideal ones we can vent to or even gain from. Communication is still multilinear and goes both ways between the sender and the receiver. Our stories, then, in a therapy point of view, do not need to be more compelling than the next person's story. They are important to us and we seek people who will validate that.

Just a quick note: Always remember that self-respect is power. Never let someone hurt you and feel satisfied. Just know he or she will not get away with it. The person lost you by disregarding you. We are all rough around the edges. No one is ideally imperfect and that does not mean anything specifically *bad*. If we frame *rough around the edges* more as anticipating or encompassing flaws, we run into negative representation of those edges and do not want to embrace them. That is why my call to action is this: reframe or recontextualize them. They are not flaws; they are idiosyncrasies or subtleties. Reframing them will help you love and respect yourself more comprehensively. You are fully enabled and fully ennobled. Remember to reaffirm you are loved, foremost by you; that carries significant, nonnegotiable weight.

Just another quick note: I can cite therapy as being transformative, but does it really render us changed people when we undergo it?

It is life-changing. To what extent is it life-changing other than transcending our imposed barriers and expanding our horizons and cognitions?

The Power of Habit

I can personally attest to this idea. A habit of thinking positively clouds and reduces negative thinking. Negative thinking is perilous and undesirable, especially when we are looking to avoid pits of depression and dejection.

Things That Cloud Judgment

Judgment is a term associated with facetious ideas like "throwing shade" or being a gossip. We may have unfortunately reduced the term in importance, when it is important just to stress how significant it is. We need our judgment, and we need to trust it and rely on it. As such, we need to make sure it is not clouded or shrouded. There are items that can cloud our judgment.

1. Overthinking: Overthinking a situation blocks us from viewing the bigger picture of the situation, its intricacies and its ramifications. We become impetuous, stressed, and presumptuous, fabricating scenarios with our loved ones or the people in our life. This will only lead to being beleaguered by and preoccupied with projected and petty ideals. This adds unnecessary and/or indiscriminate weight to an issue, often complicating it and causing it to be misperceived. It causes thoughts to build upon each other and worry us further.
2. Jumping to conclusions: This is a side effect of overthinking, as I indicated previously. Jumping to conclusions is detrimental to our sanity and clouds our clarity. It causes us to hover over minute things that should not concern us.

44

3. Narrowmindedness: Being myopic, narrow-minded, and/ or shortsighted causes us also to lose sight or track of a situation. We fail to see any picture here. We need to keep an open mind to approach a situation comprehensively and agreeably.

4. Mental fatigue: I do not think we use this term often enough, when it is a very real phenomenon. We can be miserly when it comes to thinking. As much as we want to doubt it, thinking can be exhausting. In the world we live in, thinking can be coupled with anxiety and/or negativity. That is why we have to focus on positive thoughts and curb excessive ruminating on what we cannot control. This will help us avoid or reduce mental fatigue or chances of it.

Tone and Mood

When speaking to someone, it is important to be mindful of tone. Tone, to me, is what sets the mood and climate of communication. It dictates the flow of the dialogue. Tone can be used to placate someone or used to assert oneself, thus making the communication stronger with conviction. When one wants to convey sentiments of less intensity, the tone will take a subtler form and be manifest in a different way.

If context can have a tremendous impact on tone, like where you are and/or what time of day it is, tone has to signal clear intention. This will keep us focused, even if it is morning and we are cranky, or trying to seem professional in a job interview.

In therapy, your tone can take numerous courses and forms. In therapy, there is more leeway for tone to waver and transform. That is strictly therapy. When you are speaking to a peer, you may be providing therapy, and you will pay attention to the way the mood or tone is set.

Doing Your Best

Always remember that your best is *yours*, not anyone else's. It can be met with hostility, and this should not be projected onto you. It is human nature to chastise that best, and more than one person will not have the same idea of your best as you do. It will always be highly subjective, but it should never be problematic. Your best is simply the effort you are putting forth.

Your best is not uniform; it changes. It changes from context to context and task to task. It is not tedious or unchanging; as opposed to that, it changes in namely that intensity and effort of the best you give. It is dictated by conditions and settings, but ultimately your best is your best. You make it what it is by putting forth the effort you feel to be necessary and the intensity you are harboring or channeling into it. For example, your best on a standardized test will be different from your best at your favorite sport. You will likely expend more effort at perfecting your dunks and range on your long two-point shots because you enjoy the sport of basketball. Studying for the LSAT is a nondescript, arduous task that offers not as much leeway or flexibility as a cultivated, familiar, and mobilizing activity like basketball. Some activities are just more hermetic and offer different opportunities for growth. Sure, studying for law school admission will ultimately equip you with knowledge and aptitude but in drastically different ways than sports or reading your favorite author.

Keep in mind how your best is susceptible to being chastised and/ or even berated. You know you cannot make everyone happy, even when you are trying your best. Remember that the other person or people do not know you are putting your best foot forward. They might be seeing your effort as lackluster and may not know how much effort or passion is in your work.

Good and Bad Baggage

Histories are fraught and irrevocable; they are weighted with traumas, influences, good baggage, and bad baggage. The good baggage is beneficial and constructive, while the bad baggage is impeding and hindering. We all have stories and have embarked on countless adventures, whether intentionally or unintentionally. The stories consist of histories that impacted them and still impact them. Histories are concrete and undeniable; we must learn to live with them, whether they include sins or regrets we disdain from the past or a family history of bipolar disorder. We prepare ourselves to deal with them and improve ourselves in the process.

Some baggage comes in the form of banalities that we carry and that are more weighted than we believe them to be. One of these is language. It is used arbitrarily and unfairly to terrorize us. The concept that language transcends borders is anything but prosaic. Language proves that boundaries and borders are non-existent and are constructed. It proves that they only are theoretical and notional and are meant to be crossed and passed.

I know I started off talking about language, but it related heavily to borders. Just like we have a virtually borderless, transitional, globalizing world where borders are more mechanically imposed than natural, language travels across these borders/boundaries. Language helps us look into what I will coin as cultural mirrors. The ideals that cohere in the vast world can be culturally tinged. The culturally tinged concepts and ideas in our world help us align with our cultures and languages. Gloria Anzaldúa said language is a part of us, and when attacked, hurts our sense of self. She relates it to being afraid of being censured.[38] The cultural mirror is when one who speaks our language directly resonates with us. Language is borderless and surpasses borders and boundaries and even the ideas of them. It is good baggage, even beneficial baggage. This overlaps with being of Pakistani heritage. In addition to English, I grew up speaking Urdu.

---

[38] Gloria Anzaldúa, *Borderlands/La Frontera: The New Mestiza* (San Francisco, CA: Aunt Lute Books, 1987), 75.

When a Pakistani person claims he or she cannot speak Urdu, it saddens me a bit.

When it comes to boundaries, it is advisable and wise to learn how to give people the benefit of the doubt. Life is hectic enough. You do not want to invite baggage haphazardly and aimlessly into your life. You have a win-win situation and keep sanity as a bonus. You keep people in your life. Setting boundaries is key to keeping the people in your life who require those boundaries. Boundaries are often taken as dismissive and become reasons people are irked. They feel unwanted. Boundaries are actually ways for people to invite you into their lives in more profound and nuanced ways.

Turning Weakness into Strength

It is important for a person to view his or her weaknesses as strengths. Do not be daunted; carry yourself with conviction and poise. Be ardent, adamant, and resolute in how your assert yourself, verbally or nonverbally. To overcome seeing yourself as a weak victim, you can practice a few changes and apply them regularly:

1. Do not draw pity to yourself. Do not self-pity or self-deprecate. Seeing yourself as a small person will become habitual. That is undesirable.
2. Keep pushing forward in life. Hone a focal point that motivates and moves you. Focus on it.
3. Do not think negatively. This is easier said than done, and it takes practice. However, one of my main visions for this book is that you will be dissuaded from and unaccustomed to doing just that. As humans, we induce anxiety in ourselves by thinking of worst-case scenarios instead of better ones. I know when I stopped doing this, I gained peace within myself. I stopped viewing myself as a victim of the scenario and more or less as the winner. Trust me, this works. I

stopped the incessant and unbridled anxiety that used to eat at me.

4. Do not let setbacks deter you. In time, you will not view them as setbacks.

Personal Values

One needs to have values that are open. They need to be evolutionary, not myopic or dead-ended. It will help a person to have and project these values, and ideally, they are progressive and forward-thinking. Values will inevitably be projected onto peers, but this depends on intensity and closeness. Values can be positive or negative and can be projected positively or negatively. They closer two people are or a group is, the more susceptible they are to projecting values onto one another.

I also would like to insert a cheesy *Star Wars* reference in here about the light side and dark side. I postulate that it is important to embrace and balance both. They are naturally and profusely intertwined. This means we can select beneficial facets from both and control them according to the balance we need to keep.

The Act of Unhealing

Is it ever ideal to "unheal"—that is, to undo our healing and open our wounds? Isn't there something therapeutic about opening our metaphorical bandages, being vulnerable, and sharing our stories, mainly to help others heal? Our traumas are advantageous, maybe not to ourselves but to others, and not in hostile ways. Our traumas are resonant, teachable, and illuminating even though they are in no way desirable. Our traumas shouldn't be reclusive. Yes, we have ideally healed from them, but we can share them positively with an ailing world to mitigate the collective agony plaguing and confronting us.

Healing, as we evidently see, occurs in myriad forms and contexts. Unhealing, when externally motivated, is usually negative. We need to find the unhealing in ourselves and it will lead to more profound healing.

Unhealing is basically opening your wounds. You become *vulnerable* enough to share the histories and facets of the wounds. You use them to spread insight and gifts that keep on giving. Unhealing *is* telling your story.

Bucket Lists

I originally planned for this to be a small aside, but you will see why it grew to be a subsection in the book. The fact is that we subconsciously carry bucket lists with us. We use them as guides for life. We want to accomplish or simply enact things in life, and that's what we document in bucket lists.

Bucket lists, however, are also both reminders of our mortality ways to immortalize that mortality. We can accomplish many things with our bucket lists and even scrapbook them. This way, we leave imprints and footprints on this planet. Bucket lists represent the fact the we are mortal. We may not, sadly, even get to achieve everything we envision achieving. Nonetheless, bucket lists can point to what we do achieve and celebrate. Bucket lists are built upon as mortal life progresses.

Survivors: All of Us

No matter how entitled, privileged, hard-working, or productive a person may be, that person is a survivor, just like you and just like me. We are all survivors of all kinds. I am not justifying chasing privilege here, and that is a fraught conversation piece for a different focus. Surviving the chase of anything becomes engrained and evident. Some are survivors in a more literal sense, for example, survivors of suicide. Some people are survivors of that, and then not all of us are. All of us have trauma, and this trauma is more difficult to locate in our lives as the lifespan progresses, making trauma recessive but obtrusive.

The reason I began this section including entitled or privileged people in this conversation is that struggles are still struggles, no matter how we deal with them or how equipped we are to deal with them. Sometimes, the resources do not have a hierarchy.

Artifacts: Remnants of the Future

The title of this subsection may seem outlandish, mainly because it is oxymoronic. We know artifacts are from the past. I am calling for us to look at artifacts more widely and progressively. Artifacts indicate transcendence and transience. We go in and out of worlds and realms from which we retrieve these artifacts. They help us unlock intuitions and indicators of the future. The past may be past, but the future resembles artifacts of the past.

Our Focus

We need a clear-sighted, unique narrative that presents forward-thinking and actionable models of thinking, evaluating, perceiving, and feeling. We need to focus more on avoiding mistakes that have happened and that exist around us, ranging from the most evident or conspicuous mistakes to the most subtle.

We may ask where we are headed as a world. This is a broad question that requires an answer on varying levels and possibly on a spectrum. We can learn from the past, but that is cliché. We should also place focus on the present and learning from current affairs. When we learn from the present, we observe how societies and the world globalize and trickle around us with a domino effect and influence each other. Societies differ in how they tell us about the world at large and on a micro level as well.

To be focused on more positive ideals, we should look at how the world is increasingly progressive and loving, because it is. We do not need to draw pity to us because the world is referred to as broken and decrepit.

Steps Forward

It is obvious that we cannot live in a mind state that deems the world an uninhabitable, fragmented space. The world is expansive, and so is the future. We need to start from lower levels and build up to larger levels, confronting the systemic failures and disadvantages of societies, states, countries, and the world.

We cannot afford to fall into traps with our mental health. Mental health is important, because poor mental health evolves into downward spirals, like addictions.

Final Thoughts

"Youth is wasted on the young" is a common phrase. This does not mean youth is disposable. Youth is always in us, which reminds me of my uncle Walt Disney.

In his book *The Dictionary of Obscure Sorrows*, John Koenig claims that adolescence is the height of life or emotion. It is a fable, but heights (peaks and valleys) are equally achievable at any point in life.[39]

It is said that time has healing potential and healing mechanisms. While that is true, we should remember that healing is up to us. The great part is that time is a bonus; we do not need to trade anything for it because it is there. Time is hard to describe, but maybe what we need is clarity working in unison with time to get us contentment.

---

[39] Koenig, John. *Dictionary of Obscure Sorrows* (New York, NY: Simon & Schuster, 2021.), 161.

GLOSSARY OF THERAPY/
CREATIVE TERMS

Some words and concepts carry significant weight and drastically different meanings for therapy patients and also for creatives. For creatives, language and rules are codified. There are codes and cultures. This glossary tackles the words and concepts that are treated differently in therapeutic writing and in the creative world. It also contains the phrases and terms that are contextualized differently or viewed differently by creatives. All of the words here may not occur or recur in the book, but they are therapy words. This list is exhaustive and definitions are typically my original takes and definitions on the terms, so this is not a traditional glossary.

Aesthetics: Aesthetics is often conflated with beauty. However, aesthetics is a broad and expansive field, maybe even ambiguous but surely subjective. It is an umbrella term for everything we marvel at, whether it is art, fashion, beauty, nature, or something else.

Aspiration(s): I used to conflate this word with goals, but I realize it is contextually more meaningful. Sure, an aspiration is a goal, but it is a *dream*. It is what we envision and may have always envisioned.

Catharsis: Catharsis is not as rooted, grounded, or difficult as healing. It is a result of healing and is an intangible, invisible phenomenon. Healing is as well, but catharsis is more so.

Camaraderie: Everyone is intertwined and involved in a connection that is mutual. It is based on exchange; it is both concrete and abstract.

Co-dependence: This word may invoke images of alcoholic partners, but the definition has expanded. Denotatively, a co-dependent person relies on a partner who needs support. Co-dependence is a cycle.

It is hard to get out of, and it implicates that you need help. When being with a reliant, unstable person, you run the risk of becoming so yourself.

Codes: Codes exist in language, art, fashion, popular culture, media, communication, literature, and so on. They can sometimes be vernacular and endemic to a society. They govern how we interact, but do not limit us. Codes are inscribed in society; we make them and have always made them, subconsciously. Some codes are generational—there is a gap between generations who do not understand each others' codes. Codes annoy us at times, but some are beneficial. An example is slowing at yellow lights or giving pedestrians the right of way. Barcodes are codes, but that is more literal than what I am going for here.

Culture: Culture is composed of codes and mores. Cultures can be religious, regional, philosophic (identifying as a stoic or skeptic), or related to fashion (mod, punk, and the like).

Epiphany: An epiphany is a profound and sudden realization—at least that is how I define it. Originally used to describe a religious or scientific breakthrough, we can easily say it has expanded its roots and definition. Epiphanies are naturally cathartic and demarcate transformation.

Future: The future is multilayered and multilateral. It has multiple sides and facets. It can be realistic or fantasized and fetishized. In therapy and for innovative and imaginative people, it is weighted and poses opportunities and obstacles. The important thing to note (especially for a creative) is that the future is yours and is in your hands. It is yours to experiment with, shape, imagine, create, and manipulate. This is where the possibilities are endless.

Gaslighting and self-gaslighting: These are related to toxicity and self-toxicity. Gaslighting is when one is manipulated into questioning if he or she is sane. Sanity becomes an uncertainty in this scenario. Self-gaslighting arose in a social media post, and I began to look into it. A person can manipulate himself or herself to a point where the person questions his or her sanity. It is more weighted but equally real. A person questions his or her confidence and sanity to a point where he or she represses emotion. This results from being gaslighted, and the extrinsic thoughts become internalized. For example, "It's all in your head" becomes "It's all in my head." See how that is unhealthy?

Goals: Approaching goals step-by-step, with baby steps, is vital. We all have goals; they are subjective to our individual selves, yet they do not define us. Goals represent our moods, our roles in the world, our purposes, and the meaning of our lives. We ambitiously chase both short-term and long-term goals. We invest time, money, and our physical selves into goals, so they need to be balanced with our well-being.

Healing: Healing can be confused with catharsis, but I assure you they differ. Healing is a process and so is catharsis, but catharsis is less visible. Healing is part of the journeys we are on. Healing happens in various ways and can occupy us all differently. Healing can be a complicated and possibly transcendent process. It can be difficult due to conditions you are in, environments that surround you, and people who surround you as well. Healing can be immensely personal and individualistic, but it is a collectivistic process when done in groups or when sharing your story.

Identification: Identification, in the most rudimental sense, is how a being is recognized. It can also mean the ways in which a person is characterized. Identification is important because it is how one person sees another person. It speaks to a person's traits and which distinguish him or her.

Improvement: We have all heard the overdone cliché "There's always room for improvement." How much bearing does this really have, especially when it is said and heard so often?

Innovation: Innovation is often synonymous with creativity. It measures our capacity to be creative and imaginative. In another denotative sense, it is a product of our imagination, no matter what it is. It should be something we are proud of and that motivates us to continue our journeys.

Interdependence: This is an interaction or interactions. I have always thought of this word as repetitive because interdependence means relying on others, however, so does dependence. This word means that two parties or entities are involved and depend on one another. This is so awe-inspiring to have. Two or more people supporting each other is amazing, and sometimes that support is what we most need to prevent us from wilting or going awry.

Intimacy: This term is more meaningful in therapy and for the creative person. It is not intimacy in the physical sense, but encompasses the intangible facets of closeness.

Journey: This definition is fraught and subjective, chiefly because we are all on our own journeys. It is counterproductive to judge one's journey or approach it in a hostile manner. We all need to support each other in our journeys throughout life. A journey can take a long time to define, so I will touch on the most important facets of the journey. The journey constitutes the person on the journey and the person lives the journey. It becomes familiar but at the same time progressively challenging. The journey introduces the person to new sides of people and places and abstract and concrete things. The journey is full of revelations and epiphanies.

Language: Language is how we communicate. It can be verbal or nonverbal. It can be expressions, symbols, manipulations, or cues.

Meaning: Meaning is ever-present and impactful, especially for those who are in therapy. It is inherent and engrained in everything and anything but has boundless importance and substance. For creatives, it can be made and manipulated. A permeable and malleable entity, it is an outlet for emotion in several ways. Meaning animates the inanimate, as necessitated by our mental states. It can be deeper or shallower, but it always has a uniquely high bearing on life and condition.

Media: The media plays an imperative role in our mental health. It can have negative facets as well as positive ones.

Mindfulness: Mindfulness means living in the present and being aware and in control of your thoughts, insights, dispositions, and emotions.

Needs: For this, I highly encourage you to refer to Abraham Maslow's hierarchy of needs. My take on needs is they are endless and ever-present. Our needs are the basics that we acquire, like food and water and shelter. Maslow also lists self-actualization as a need. Self-actualization is overlooked and not given the magnitude of attention it calls for and deserves. Self-actualization involves unlocking and thus reaching one's potential. In this context, the creative potential is unlocked. The motivation or drive that this necessitates is coherent. It flows and ebbs and needs to be *unlocked*.

Self-efficacy: The most relatable term to this is *confidence*. When you get your creative juices flowing, you become unstoppable. You can unlock confidence and feel self-sufficient. You are adequate. Self-efficacy is an assessment of the confidence that will enable your ultimate goals and aspirations to come true. Your motivation and environment interact. It can be performative in that it represents attainment of goals by your performance in the world at large.

Self-esteem: We all have self-esteem. It can be agonizing to keep it high, I attest, but it can also be euphoric and rewarding to have high self-esteem. Low self-esteem is counter to therapeutic feeling. Self-esteem causes one to not fall below a threshold of certainty and trust in the self.

Self-identification: Self-identification is a person's self-concept. This is not only the attributes individuals give themselves, but it is deeply rooted in the self-concept. It is rooted in how one sees himself or herself. The self is central and becomes more focal than anything, as it should be. This should not just answer "Who am I?" but go beyond and answer "Why am I?" (as in "Why am I here?"). This question puzzles me but I find it satisfying when I dig out an appropriate answer. The fact that this question can be posed to you means inherently that you have a purpose and a meaning.

Success: You can recontextualize and redefine success. It is subjective, highly personal, and malleable.

Support: Support is (at least to me) the most important word I have included here. This is because it is what we need. I can seldom function without some type of support. I don't need people always around me, but I am an extrovert. I gain energy from people and feel it. When one has support, it makes a tremendous difference. Support is greatest when *always* felt. It can be disembodied when talking about mental health. Sometimes relying on one's innovative side is a support that makes us feel self-sufficient.

Support system: This can be vast and expansive or minute and small. However small, it is not limited. It occurs in all sizes and multiplicities. A support system can also benefit from being smaller.

Transcendence: This word describes such ideals as healing and catharsis. For me, this speaks about our globalized, borderless world, and reminds me that ideas and cultures migrate and interact.

Technology has evolved, benefitted, and sometimes impeded media and media has entwined with it.

Ubiquity: This term relates to universality and actualization. It could be related to, maybe even conflated with, the oversoul.

Utopia: Usually, we say utopia is idyllic; it is how we want to live. Oxford Reference defines the utopia as "an imagined place or state of things in which everything is perfect."[40] This invokes another thinker for me, Benedict Anderson. He talks about imagined communities, where we support each other and where homogeneity is valid. He encourages solidarity and talks about the conflict between nationalism and a borderless world.[41]

Voice: Voice has to be amplified. Voice is not visible—or is it? We protest and congregate with voice. Voice is a corollary to creativity and a monumental form of self-support. Voice manifests itself in many ways and begs to be heard.

[40] "Utopia," *Oxford Reference,* accessed November 30, 2022, https://www.oxfordreference.com/view/10.1093/oi/authority.20110803115009560.
[41] Benedict Anderson. *Imagined Communities: Reflections on the Origin and Spread of Nationalism* (London, UK: Verso books, 2006), 223.

BIBLIOGRAPHY

Adler, Ronald, Rosenfeld, Lawrence, and Proctor II, Russell. *Interplay.* New York, NY: Oxford University Press, 2010.

Allers, Roger and Rob Minkoff, dir. *The Lion King.* 1994; Burbank, CA: Buena Vista Pictures, 2003. DVD.

Anderson, Benedict. *Imagined Communities: Reflections on the Origin and Spread of Nationalism* (London, UK: Version Books, 2006.)

Anzaldúa, Gloria. *Borderlands/La Frontera: The New Mestiza.* San Francisco, CA: Aunt Lute Books, 1987.

Chomsky, Noam. *Reflections on Language.* Cambridge, MA: Temple Smith, 1976.

Cockerell, Lee, and Jody Mayberry. "How to Be a Better Listener." *Creating Disney Magic.* Podcast audio. August 2021. https://open.spotify.com/episode/1awnQSBb9QmVtFBhkIhYeW.

Cockerell, Lee and Mayberry, Jody. "You've Got to Know More to Be More." *Creating Disney Magic.* Podcast audio. July 2021. https://open.spotify.com/show/6ThERLxDTQlf16TBNyVPPS.

Debord, Guy. *The Society of the Spectacle.* Paris, France: Black and Red, 1967.

Ford, Thompson Richard. *Dress Codes: How the Laws of Fashion Made History.* New York: Simon and Schuster, 2021.

Friends. 1997. Season 4 Episode 3, "The One with the Cuffs." Directed by Pete Bonerz. Aired October 9, 1997 on KTLA.

Gabler, Neal. *Walt Disney: The Triumph of the American Imagination.* New York: Vintage, 2006.

Gabriel, Mike and Eric Goldberg, dir. *Pocahontas.* 1995; Burbank, CA: Buena Vista Pictures, 2000. DVD.

Geertz, Clifford. "Deep play: Notes on the Balinese cockfight." *Daedalus* 101, no. 1 (1972): 1-37.

Hebdige, Dick. "The Unnatural Break." In *Media and Cultural Studies*, ed. Meenakshi Gigi Durham and Douglas M. Kellner (New York NY: Wiley, 2001), 144.

Heider, Karl G. "What Do People Do? Dani Auto-Ethnography." *Journal of Anthropological Research*. 31, no. 1 (Spring 1975): 3–17.

Koenig, David. *Mouse Under Glass: Secrets of Disney Animation and Theme Parks*. Irvine, CA: Bonaventure Press, 2015.

Koenig, John. *The Dictionary of Obscure Sorrows*. Simon and Schuster, 2021.

Lucas, George, dir. *Star Wars Episode I: The Phantom Menace*. 1999; Los Angeles, CA: 20th Century Fox, 2005. DVD.

Lucas, George, Dir. *Star Wars Episode II: Attack of the Clones*. 2002; Los Angeles, CA: 20th Century Fox, 2002. DVD.

Luvaas, Brent. *Street Style: An Ethongraphy of Fashion Blogging*. London: Bloomsbury Academic, 2016.

Marquand, Richard, dir. *Star Wars Episode VI: The Return of the Jedi*. 1983; Los Angeles, CA: 20th Century Fox, 2005. DVD.

Maslow, Abraham, and Lewis, K. J. "Maslow's Hierarchy of Needs." *Salenger Incorporated* 14, no. 17 (1987): 987-990.

Merleau-Ponty, Maurice, and John F. Bannan. "What is phenomenology?" *CrossCurrents* 6, no. 1 (1956): 59-70.

Petryszak, Nicholas G. "Tabula rasa–its origins and implications." *Journal of the History of the Behavioral Sciences* 17, no. 1 (January 1981): 15-27.

Seelig, Tina. "A Crash Course in Creativity." Filmed August 2012 at TEDxStanford, Stanford, CA. Video, 18:15. https://www.youtube.com/watch?v=gyM6rx69iqg.

Smith, Cherise. "Cultural Appropriation is Everywhere. But Is it Always Wrong?" *Time*, September 21, 2016. https://time.com/4501037/cultural-appropriation-marc-jacobs-dreadlocks/.

Sontag, Susan. *Against Interpretation and Other Essays*. New York: Dell, 1966.

Thornton, Sarah. *Seven Days in the Art World*. New York: W.W. Norton and Company, 2009.

"Utopia." Oxford Reference. Accessed November 30, 2022. https://www.oxfordreference.com/view/10.1093/oi/authority.20110803115009560.

Yasin, Hasan S. "Being Innovative by Being Authentic." Filmed May 2021 at TEDxSaddarRoad, Rawalpindi, Pakistan. Video, 17:57. https://www.youtube.com/watch?v=LlNxaXsWupE.

Volk-Weiss, Brian, dir. *Behind the Attraction*. "Space Mountain." Season 1, episode 5. Aired July 21, 2021, on DisneyPlus. https://www.disneyplus.com/video/cd1da80e-09c2-4b5d-b0bc-7dd8f3be648f.

von Busch, Otto. *The Psychopolitics of Fashion: Conflict and Courage Under the Current State of Fashion*. London: Bloomsbury Visual Arts, 2020.

Printed in the United States
by Baker & Taylor Publisher Services